'TIL DEATH DO US...'

A TRUE CRIME STORY OF BIGAMY AND MURDER

PATRICK GALLAGHER

WILDBLUE
PRESS

WildBluePress.com

'TIL DEATH DO US...' published by:
WILDBLUE PRESS
P.O. Box 102440
Denver, Colorado 80250

Publisher Disclaimer: Any opinions, statements of fact or fiction, descriptions, dialogue, and citations found in this book were provided by the author, and are solely those of the author. The publisher makes no claim as to their veracity or accuracy, and assumes no liability for the content.

WILDBLUE PRESS is registered at the U.S. Patent and Trademark Offices.

ISBN 978-1-952225-16-1 Trade Paperback
ISBN 978-1-952225-15-4 eBook

Cover design © 2020 WildBlue Press. All rights reserved.

Interior Formatting/Book Cover Design by Elijah Toten
www.totencreative.com

'TIL DEATH
DO US...'

TABLE OF CONTENTS

AUTHOR'S NOTE

The lead defense attorney in this case, Patrick Joseph (PJ) Gallagher was my grandfather, and I had the great fortune to grow up as a little boy living right next door to him and my grandmother, Florence, who went by Patsy. Granddad was a larger than life figure, and many in the family wanted to be named after him.

Born November 4, 1884, PJ was 62 years old at the time of the Broadhurst Trial. The process he underwent to become an attorney illuminates his personality perfectly. About the time my grandmother was expecting their second child in 1909, PJ realized he could not support a family on wages as a cowhand, so he determined to become an attorney. At that time in South Dakota a person could become an attorney after three years of apprenticeship in a law office and successfully passing the bar exam. PJ arranged a position as an apprentice, but was having an extremely difficult time supporting his young family on the meager wages earned as an apprentice. After six months he approached his supervising attorney and urged him to write Pierre, the state capital, to tell them he had served one year of apprenticeship. After much badgering and insisting he had learned in six months what the average apprentice would in a year, the attorney sent the letter. After another very difficult year trying to make ends meet, he suggested to his mentor that he write a letter to Pierre declaring Patrick Gallagher to be a hardship case, requesting permission for him to take the bar exam one year early. The attorney vigorously objected, reminding PJ he had only been apprenticing one and a half years, not two. Again, after much cajoling and urging, the attorney assented, being sure the request would be denied, but at least it would get PJ off his back. To his surprise, the request was granted. PJ went to Pierre about a week prior to the date of the exam and spent that week hanging out in the bar near the capitol building which was most often frequented by the attorneys. The capitol building also housed the state supreme court. Perhaps PJ heard the bar exam discussed among them as they lingered over their drinks, perhaps not. The result was, however, that PJ passed the exam and was admitted to the bar in South Dakota as an attorney on October 16, 1911. By that time, he had three children; my father, Martin Patrick Gallagher, being the third child in a family that would later grow to five children.

My father, known as Buck, also became an attorney and he and PJ practiced law together in Ontario, Oregon at the time of the Broadhurst trial. Dad was a State Representative in the Oregon Legislature at the time of the trial, and was unable to participate in the trial to any large extent. In 1999, I asked my mother about her recollections of this trial, and she remembered it vividly. Even after more than 50 years, she was quite piqued that Dad had forbidden her to attend the trial. I'm not quite sure why Dad did this, perhaps he thought it too lurid for his young wife.

I remember Jordan Valley well, as my father had a number of clients among the residents of that area, most of them Basques, and he travelled to that area often. Ontario and the surrounding region had a large population of Basques, and I attended school and played with many of them. They are wonderful people that anyone would be proud to know and have for friends. One of Dad's college roommates was a Basque man named Tony Yturri, and he and his wife, Remi, were some of the finest people I have known. Tony was also an attorney, but he spent his career in politics as a State Senator in Oregon. Dad said he could easily have been governor if he wasn't from the far eastern edge of the state.

The contested will of Dr. Broadhurst was a big news item around that country, and of course most folks thought it a travesty that Gladys was able to receive anything at all out of the estate.

Granddad died on May 8, 1957, about 10 months after Gladys was paroled. I have no information about any further contact between them, nor what he thought of Gladys Broadhurst personally. Having been related to a number of attorneys, it has always been interesting to me how they handle representing a client they know, or are pretty certain, is guilty. Without exception, they have all told me that every defendant in America is guaranteed by law to receive a fair trial and a vigorous defense by the laws of our country. They see it as their sworn duty to provide their clients the best possible defense, without regard to their personal feelings about the individual.

<u>PROLOGUE</u>

```
TAFT, CAL 20 AUGUST 1945 1330 HRS
TO: W.D. BROADHURST, CALDWELL, IDAHO
VIA: WESTERN UNION

DEAREST BROADY: MEMORIES OF OUR
NIGHTS TOGETHER SO MANY YEARS AGO
STILL FLOOD MY DREAMS TODAY. STOP. I
HAVE NEVER FORGOTTEN YOU. STOP. HOW
COULD I EVER FORGET A MAN LIKE YOU?
STOP.
I'D LOVE TO TELL YOU MY STORY. STOP.
PLEASE WRITE WITH YOUR ADDRESS IF
INTERESTED:

GLADYS RALPHS LINCOLN
411 S 7 ST
TAFT, CA

STOP.
```

PART I - DESPERATION

CHAPTER 1

<u>May 19, 1927 – 18 Years Prior</u>

Who knows the heart of a young woman? Does even she know what motivates her, what drives her passions, what desires and fears compete within her?

Gladys June Ralphs, 20 years old and living in Minidoka, Idaho, which at the time of her marriage boasted a whopping citizenry of 200 souls, was beautiful and headstrong. She thought she knew her mind. She was sure she was ready to step out from under the wings of her parents William and Anna. The "middle" of five children, Gladys was also the only girl. She really loved her brothers, and they doted over her as well. Affectionately nicknamed "Flea" by the brothers, they were always there for her whenever she got into trouble. And that she did in abundance!

As was typical in faithful Mormon families, they all had strong family feelings and each of the boys married well, and for life. That is why it is so strange that Gladys did not fit the mold. Where they were strong, she was weak. They made their faith a central part of their everyday lives. Gladys used her LDS connections as a tool to achieve her goals. She lived within the circle of Mormonism, but it was never a significant influence in her decision making.

What did influence the decision making of Gladys Ralphs?

Jesse was the oldest and three years older. Eugene was two years older and carried the nickname "Red." Sterling Anthony, who went by "Tony," was two years younger. The baby of the family, Clifford, was called "Bud" or "Buddy" by everyone. A great family ... but a tragedy in the making, for Gladys was always a worry, always in crisis.

Was it something the family did wrong in the way they raised Gladys? Was it some inherited flaw that came down from some ancient unknown ancestor? Perhaps just raising a daughter is just way different than bringing up those rowdy boys, and her parents missed the difference. The folks certainly loved Gladys just as much as the boys, perhaps even more because she was the only girl. And maybe that was part of the problem.

Possibly some of the problem was the way they always bailed her out whenever a situation arose. Somewhere the notion that a person learns from the consequences they encounter is negated when the consequences don't really touch them. Can it be that a shielded life is actually great harm to the child and her proper development? When parents are trying their best to do what is right, sometimes they bend over backwards too far and they actually create the very evil they are trying to overcome.

Gladys June Ralphs married William Bacel Hendricks on May 19 of 1927, a few weeks before her twenty-first birthday. Gladys did not have a middle name according to her birth certificate, but she felt that a middle name sounded more auspicious, and June struck her as a good one. Short and easy to pronounce, it added a certain dignity and refinement to her given name. Of course, she became Gladys Hendricks when she married William, but unfortunately the marriage didn't last, nor did the name. After she and William divorced less than a year after their wedding day, Gladys reverted to her maiden name.

CHAPTER 2

The average person might assume that such a disastrous marriage that ended so quickly and abruptly would cause someone to think twice about jumping right back into the frying pan immediately. But perhaps the frying pan was the whole cause of the problem with the first marriage. Had Gladys strayed from her marriage vows? Was infidelity the cause of the sudden end to her first marriage? Is that why Gladys' second marriage on August 6, 1928 was so soon after her first? The second wedding was only 14 months after her marriage to Hendricks.

Gladys listed on her marriage license to marry Albert Earnest Richardson that she was "single," as was Albert. They were married in Logan, Utah, but took up residence in Burley, Idaho where Albert worked as a railroad clerk. But a marriage initiated by infidelity is not likely to succeed, and such was the case with Gladys and Albert and their marriage. By March 1931, Gladys is mentioned on the society page in the *Nevada State Journal* newspaper as "Miss Gladys Ralphs," who "is in Sacramento where she will spend several weeks." Thus, it appears the second marriage, including the second married name, lasted less than two and a half years.

Further, we later will learn that during her time living in Burley, Gladys developed a "sweetheart," a young doctor of Chiropractic, Willis David Broadhurst. W.D., as he was fond to be addressed, had graduated from the Palmer School for Chiropractic Medicine in Davenport, Iowa in 1924 and had established his medical practice in Burley shortly thereafter. He treated Gladys when she and Albert lived in Burley and they developed a romantic interest in each other, despite the fact that he was 11 years older. It is very possible that this relationship hastened the end of Gladys' second marriage, and it definitely resulted in W.D. moving from Burley to Caldwell, Idaho to re-establish his medical practice anew.

After the demise of her second marriage, Gladys spent the next seven years unmarried. During that time, she toured with her family and sang with their band, known as "The Ralphs Novelty Orchestra." All of the family had talent, particularly Gladys who could play the piano and accordion and had a marvelous singing voice. Her voice was often compared with the young film and song star Deanna Durbin, and many said her voice and her beauty were equal to that of Miss Durbin.

And perhaps here we find a kernel of understanding into the psyche and actions of Gladys Ralphs. Why is it that such talent so often carries with it an extra measure of emotional challenges? Why do special abilities carry special burdens? Does God give such people their "thorn in the flesh" to help keep them humble? If humility was typically the result of such pain, we would agree with this conclusion. But so often it is not humility but anger, hurt and depression that dog the footsteps of peculiarly talented people.

The time spent with her family touring and singing was good for Gladys, and being talented and attractive she enjoyed much attention from the men she met, so she wasn't really lonely. But none of these relationships worked out. Was it the men? Or was there something in Gladys that torched the relationships? Some men only want to take advantage, but often it was Gladys who couldn't commit to a strong, permanent relationship. We hear so often about men who are unfaithful and don't stay true to their pledge to be true, but Gladys was equally guilty of having a roving eye. For her, the excitement was in the conquest, the challenge was to have the power to bend men to her will. Once she succeeded, her attention was drawn to the next man.

CHAPTER 3

The next man was Carroll M. Anderson, who at 31 years of age was a year younger than Gladys (although she listed her age on the marriage license as 30, shaving a couple years off the truth). Gladys was living in Sacramento at the time they married on January 30, 1939. She also decided on a new middle name, thinking "Elaine" sounded a little more sophisticated.

After they married, the new couple moved into Carroll's home in Westwood, California, which was the home of the new campus of the University of California at Los Angeles (UCLA) which had been completed only 13 years earlier.

For Gladys, the move from the small town of Burley, Idaho to Sacramento had been quite exhilarating. From the flat, sagebrush and farming area with a population of about 5,000, she now lived and moved in the bustling capital city of California that swelled at the seams with over 105,000 residents. Due to being the center of the California gold rush a half century earlier, Sacramento had grown fast. Due to being the state capital, it was a beehive of activity. Gladys loved it. She loved the rivers, the rains which were more frequent than in Idaho, and the activity. There was so much to do in Sacramento, but her main goal was a man, and when she and Carroll married, she loved even more moving to Westwood.

Westwood was to die for! Adjacent to Beverly Hills, a quick drive to Santa Monica and the ocean and within striking distance from downtown Los Angeles, Gladys could imagine no more wonderful place to live than Westwood.

What a wonderful place to live. And the men. There were a lot of men in Westwood!

Westwood had been established in 1913 to be the operations center of the Red River Lumber Company, the "largest electric sawmill of the time," and that was where Carroll worked. The Red River Lumber Company was the most modern sawmill in the world, building their own railroad system to move logs from the forests to the mill. The company was also the origin of the stories of Paul Bunyan and his famous Blue Ox, Babe. These stories, written by William Laughead, were purchased by the company and published "Introducing Mr. Paul Bunyan of Westwood, California" as an advertising pamphlet in 1916.

Being a company town, most of the residents of Westwood either worked in the mill, supported the mill, or provided services to the millworkers and their families. It was a time and place where you could tell a man's occupation simply by observing how he dressed. Lumberjacks wore flannel shirts (usually with a checkerboard design), Levi jeans with big, wide, red suspenders, corked boots, and floppy red felt hats. Often the men would wear their corks as they walked down the sidewalk. There was something satisfying about hearing the click of the caulks as they rattled on the walk. These guys were the toughest.

The sawmill workers also often wore suspenders, but their clothing was typically lighter, as it could get really hot inside the mill at times. Many of them wore bib overalls, and often they wore shoes rather than boots. The mill workers were plenty tough as well. When you spend all day, every day pulling green chain, you get strong and tough or you get out. This is no work for sissies.

Gladys had no use for sissies. She liked big, strong men. Men with muscle. She liked a man who could pick her up with one arm and carry her across the threshold. And that is the kind of man Carroll was. It's just that there were so many others just as strong, just as attractive. Gladys felt like a kid in a candy store, with no one watching. Except, Carroll was watching.

Again, Gladys and her roving eye could not sustain a permanent marriage. Within a year Gladys is divorced from Carroll, the divorce being granted in Reno. Married in Reno, divorced in Reno. Kind of a round trip, wasn't it?

CHAPTER 4

The 4th marriage of Gladys Elaine Ralphs was to Virgil D. Warner on June 9, 1940, only 16 months after her 3rd marriage. They are married at the Reno Baptist Church, so clearly Gladys is straying from her Mormon roots. Virgil, who is 28 years old and 5 years younger than Gladys, was born in South Dakota. When they got married, Virgil was living with his mother and brother in Westwood. He also is an employee of the Red River Lumber Company in Westwood.

Was Virgil a neighbor? A friend of Carroll's? Is it likely they knew each other? Whether or not Virgil and Carroll knew each other, surely, they knew fellow workers who knew them both. And surely it was quite a hot topic when Gladys divorced Carroll and married a fellow Red River employee. News travels fast, and juicy news travels like lightning. And in tight-knit communities such as Westwood, the most popular form of entertainment is gossip.

By July of the next year, 1941, Virgil and Gladys had moved to Medford, Oregon, where he continued working as a sawmill worker. Why did Virgil leave his job at the largest, most modern sawmill in the world to do the same work in a smaller mill? Was it to escape the gossip? Could it have been to escape the influence of an intrusive mother who thought she needed to continue helping her boy make the right decisions in life? Or perhaps Gladys and the mother-in-law weren't too compatible, particularly if the mother of the groom felt like this evil woman had stolen the heart of her innocent son. Or, perhaps the move was necessitated to get away from an angry ex-husband who may have vowed revenge on the wife who had the nerve to treat him exactly as she had treated his predecessor. Maybe he had forgotten the old adage that "what goes around comes around." And… maybe it was just an upward move to a better job with better hours and more pay.

Unfortunately, Gladys' 4th marriage was no more successful than the previous three. By the end of the year, after their move to Medford, Gladys had moved back to Sacramento and filed for divorce. Medford was just too small, and Virgil was just too something. Or just too not something. How can we discern the motives of a woman who marries and divorces so quickly, so frequently? What lies deep within her heart that perhaps even she cannot understand or articulate? Was her emotional maturity arrested at some teenage year? Is she perpetually 13 years old in how she deals with her decisions and with the world? Is life just a game for her?

CHAPTER 5

World War II was in full force when Gladys met the dashing Lieutenant Lincoln. He was tall, he was strong, and he was going to help save America from the tyrannical egomaniacs leading Germany, Japan, and Italy. Lincoln was a geologist by training, and had joined the army in November of 1940. He was stationed at Ft. Ord in California at the time the Japanese conducted their surprise attack on Pearl Harbor.

All of America was in a fervor of patriotic excitement after Japan attacked our country and propelled the U.S. into the war. Prior to the attack there were many in the country fighting to ensure America stayed out of a war that was none of our affair. After Pearl Harbor, few still held that attitude, but anyone who did very wisely kept it to himself. Men and women were volunteering to serve at an unprecedented rate, and those who were in the military prepared to be shipped out to join the fight. They sorted out their affairs at home, which for many men included marrying their sweethearts.

Lt. Leslie M. Lincoln had met and fallen in love with the beautiful Gladys Elaine Ralphs, and they married at Ft. Ord on January 28, 1942, less than two months after the infamous Japanese attack. It was only 19 months after her marriage to Virgil. On the marriage application he listed the 80th Ordnance Co., Ft. Ord as his place of residence. He was 24 years old, 11 years younger than Gladys. It was his first marriage. In fact, some reports suggest that Gladys was actually not free to marry yet when she married the lieutenant. Her divorce to her previous husband Virgil may not yet have been final. However, who keeps track of such things? No one seemed to know, or to care.

Gladys keeps getting older and her husbands keep getting younger. She listed her age on the marriage application as 32 when in fact she was 35. She also stated this was her second marriage, but of course it was to be her fifth. Her address is shown as 2117 O Street in Sacramento, and she stated her occupation was a teacher. Most certainly that was a lie also.

The newlyweds lived on base at Ft. Ord for a couple months, then moved to Stockton for six months. At that time, Leslie was transferred to the east coast and Gladys remained in California. She moved to Inglewood in the Los Angeles area for a brief time, then lived with Leslie's mother in Pittsburg, California for 3 months in 1943. After that, Gladys returned to living in Inglewood on her own until Leslie was discharged.

This was a heady new experience for Gladys. She was married but her husband was absent. She was free to do as she pleased, with whomever she pleased. There was no husband waiting for her at home, no one looking over her shoulder. She had about two and a half years of total freedom, with the exception of the three months she lived with her mother-in-law. Life was good, life was exciting. Life was embodied with choices that could be made entirely as she wished. Her husband's paychecks kept rolling in and she developed a keen understanding that money is the key that opens the door to happiness. She liked it.

Leslie was discharged from the Army in November of 1944, about six months before the allies declared victory over Germany and ten months prior to the final end of WWII. It does not appear that Leslie ever served overseas in his military career.

After his discharge, Leslie and Gladys moved to Taft, California and lived there until October of 1945, after which they moved to 2021 P Street in Sacramento. However, this abrupt and startling change in lifestyle was no fun for

Gladys. Now she was not free. Now she could not spend as she wished. Now happiness was elusive again, and she didn't like it.

Their marriage was also plagued with a new issue: Gladys had become a drug addict. Perhaps due to her lifestyle or possibly due to the influence of some of those she came to know in southern California, Gladys had begun taking Nembutal, a drug prescribed as a sleep aid, but in far larger doses than prescribed or recommended. The normal dose is 3 grains, which can be repeated in 6-8 hours if needed. Gladys was taking 15 to 30 grains at a time, the result being she not only slept long hours but was also really groggy a good part of the day.

Things are going badly in the Lincoln household, but these things are only the symptoms of the underlying core issue: Gladys simply can't manage the role of faithful housewife. She cannot be happy just staying true to the man sleeping on the other side of the bed. For 99 out of 100 women that is their ideal, their goal. But for Gladys, it is never enough, never satisfying, never sufficient. She is always searching for the perfect man for her, and it is never the one she currently is married to. What desperate need causes her to always look for more, to look beyond, to look for the next man?

Sometimes, however, the next man is not someone new, but someone from the past. On August 20, 1945, while Leslie and Gladys still lived in Taft, Gladys sent a telegram to her old sweetheart, W.D. Broadhurst. The telegram itself was never found, but the message is believed to be thus:

```
TAFT, CAL  20 AUGUST 1945  1330 HRS
TO: W.D. BROADHURST, CALDWELL, IDAHO
VIA: WESTERN UNION

DEAREST BROADY: MEMORIES OF OUR
NIGHTS TOGETHER SO MANY YEARS AGO
STILL FLOOD MY DREAMS TODAY. STOP. I
```

```
HAVE NEVER FORGOTTEN YOU. STOP. HOW
COULD I EVER FORGET YOU? STOP.
I'D LOVE TO TELL YOU MY STORY. STOP.
PLEASE WRITE WITH YOUR ADDRESS IF
INTERESTED:

     GLADYS RALPHS LINCOLN
     411 S 7 ST
     TAFT, CA

STOP.
```

Doctor Broadhurst's first response to Gladys was a return telegram on August 25th in which he advised her of his address. As he was just leaving for a short trip, he followed up on September 5th, 1945 with a letter. His reply to her was:

```
     Just arrived home from a vacation
and found your telegram awaiting me,
so I hurry to answer it and state that
there is no Mrs. -- hence no children.
As to any other heirs, I have none.
     Am anxiously awaiting a letter
giving me all the details of your
past, present, and future. Especially
anxious to learn about your folks as
I always thot much of them.
     Can imagine many things, but
one never knows until someone tells
the details. Anyway, am hoping for a
favorable report.
     Had hoped to be out of practice
before now, but the war came along and
took my nephew who was going to take
over so now I have been stuck for a
long time and if nothing happens I am
hoping that he will be released from
```

overseas this fall. Guess I'll have to stay with him for a year or so and then I am going to take the balance of my life in the open fooling around with the ranches and doing the many things I have always wanted to do.

Happy for all that the war seems to be over and that peace may reign again in the near future. Never was much of a person for trouble and so I have lived a life very free from it. Naturally had my little disappointments but it has never made me bitter or sour on the world in general. Brighter days are always in store and so I live every day the best I know how.

Could ask a million questions but am hoping you will write thereby answering many 'that I'll not need to answer. Better get hold of yourself and get that health that all should have.

Getting busy so shall have to run along and until I hear, I am
   Sincerely,
   Dr. W. D. Broadhurst
   "Broady"

Gladys, for whatever reason she had in her twisted logic, was making a move for her next man. Scarcely nine months after the return of her husband from active military duty, she already was planning, and those plans focused on Broadhurst. But before she could see this goal as a reality, she had to establish three things:

1. The doctor must be available

2. She must show that she is available for him

3. She must appear to have wealth so that he doesn't perceive her motivation as being after his money

These requirements could easily be achieved simply by communicating with him. Ever the direct one, Gladys composed her next letter to the doctor, in which she dealt with all three matters.

September 10, 1945
My Dear Darling Doctor Broady:
I recall with great fondness the time we spent together so many years ago. I have never forgotten you… how could I ever forget you? I am sure you have had a good life with health and happiness. Unfortunately for me, I am a widow with no children.

I hope you are well. As for me, my health is still not so good and I miss having someone like you to talk things over. If you are interested, I will be happy to write, sharing with you how my life has been since we parted.

There is absolutely no doubt in my mind that you saved my life when you treated me back in Burley almost 20 years ago, Doc. Had it not been for your great skill as a chiropractor, coupled with your deep kindness, I surely would have taken my own life then, or it would have slipped away from me of its own accord. There is no understanding the depths of despair a human being can reach, or how insurmountable is the climb out of such a pit. Yet, you were there and like an angel you reached down and lifted me out of the depths.

I have had much good fortune of late, and I would like to share in that with you, due to my deep gratitude for what you have meant to me. My dearly beloved Aunt Mary from Honolulu has recently passed away and left her wonderful fortune to me, almost three million dollars. As it is more than I have ever dreamed of owning, and more than I could possibly manage, I have determined to share a small portion with those in my life who have meant the most. I would like to provide a small gift to you. If you would like that, I will instruct my attorney to include you in the disbursement. Due to the size of the estate, I have been advised it will be some time before the legal requirements are finalized.

Please do write and let me know how you have been.

With enduring love,
Gladys

Does it seem odd that right out of the chute someone would enquire about heirs? Wouldn't that be a red flag that perhaps their motives were not of the purest sort? Gladys saw this possibility and that had a lot to do with her decision that she must appear wealthy. But maybe that wasn't even necessary. Men are famous for being obtuse, particularly when a beautiful woman is showing interest in them.

Thus, began a series of correspondence between the good doctor and the woman he had fallen in love with almost 20 years earlier. He clearly had never gotten over that feeling.

What is it about Gladys that just doesn't feel right? At first meeting her, she comes across so well. She is attractive and a good conversationalist. She is outgoing and friendly and has a winning smile. Gladys relates well with you when you first meet. However, over a period of time, as you get to know her, you realize her character is flawed. Her judgments are poor and her decision making is downright disastrous. She sounds friendly when speaking with her, but you come to understand that she is just playing a role. She really doesn't care about you or anyone else besides herself. In time you come to the conclusion that she seems to have frozen in time at about age 13, and has not matured beyond that point. She is like the character in the J.M. Barrie play, "Peter Pan, or the Boy Who Wouldn't Grow Up." It's as if Gladys refused to become an adult woman, preferring the undisciplined and carefree life of a teenager.

One oddity of Gladys' personality was perhaps a result of her inability or unwillingness to grow up. She loved the movies. Of course, many adults love going to the movie theater, but for Gladys it was like psychotherapy. She seemed so impressed by the movies, perhaps "impressionable" is more accurate. If she saw a movie she particularly liked, she would often emulate her favorite character or situation in the movie. Bette Davis and Ingrid Bergman were her idols, but she had a whole list of femme fatale actresses that she admired. Perhaps it had something to do with the war being fought at such great cost to American lives, but the movies released in the 1940's were heavy on drama and suspense.

One movie that had a powerful impact on Gladys was "Leave Her to Heaven," starring Gene Tierney as Ellen Berent who meets the novelist Richard Harlan, played by Cornel Wilde, on a train. The stunningly beautiful but psychotically jealous Ellen ultimately proposes marriage to Richard. As her jealousy causes the marriage to disintegrate, Ellen turns to murder and finally creates the ultimate revenge scenario.

At one point, Ellen is reading over Richard's shoulder as he writes his novel, as he types, "'Will you marry me?' he said."

Ellen reacts, "Oh, no!"

Richard: "No what?"

Ellen: "Good grief! 'Will you marry me?' In the first place, men never propose. They think they do, but it's really the woman."

Richard: "Who told you that, Ripley?"

Ellen: "And when men do propose, they never say, 'Will you marry me?'"

After some more discussion, Ellen asks, "How did you propose to me?"

Richard: "Uh. . . . . ."

Ellen: "You didn't, I proposed to you." (Then she grabs his face and pulls it to her and gives him a huge kiss) .... "Remember?"

The relationship between W.D. and Gladys blossomed and grew as they corresponded with each other over the next several months. It is amazing that Gladys was able to carry on this clandestine relationship without Leslie learning about it. Fortunately for Gladys, Leslie was usually at work at his new job working as a geologist for Standard Oil, working hard to establish himself as a model employee. This left the gathering of mail at the mailbox to Gladys.

It also could be that as things worsened at home, escaping for long hours to the office was a welcome relief for Leslie from the drama of marital discord at home.

Doctor Broadhurst had prospered in the 20 years since his move to Caldwell, Idaho. He had purchased a 160-acre ranch on the outskirts of Caldwell and a larger cattle ranch in Eastern Oregon near the town of Jordan Valley. He lived in the ranch house outside Caldwell with his nephew, Floyd Adams, and Floyd's wife, Lola, and their two children. The doctor leased the farmland on the Caldwell ranch to Rudolph Jestrabek, who ran it as a dairy farm.

W.D. loved ranching, and was retiring from active work as a chiropractor. His nephew, Floyd, was also a chiropractor, and had moved to Caldwell to take over the medical practice. W.D. and Floyd were only 17 years apart in age, and were quite fond of each other. W.D. particularly loved having the children in the house. LeRoy was 7 years old at the time and Trina was a toddler.

Right after New Year's Day 1946, W.D. and his sister from St. Anthony, Idaho, Sarah Allen, took an extended two-month trip together. They drove from Idaho to Phoenix, then on down to Mexico and back up through Los Angeles. During that trip, when they were in Phoenix, W.D. received a letter from Gladys. In it, Gladys listed her qualifications and proposed marriage to the doctor, who showed it to Sarah and they discussed it at length. Sarah had her doubts about the relationship, but she loved her brother too much to interfere in his personal life.

On the return trip, Sarah remained behind in Los Angeles and W.D. continued on alone, heading for Sacramento where Gladys now lived. W.D. checked into the Senator Hotel, and Gladys met him there. Later W.D. said they kissed there in the hotel, and he described that kiss to "cause my love a thousand strong flash into full blossom."

One of the key elements in Gladys' plan was to allay any fears on the doctor's part that her reason for contacting him was due to his wealth. Thus, she created the story about the death of her beloved Aunt Mary Johnson from Honolulu who had died and bequeathed her a fortune of three million dollars. She judged that if W.D. viewed her as even wealthier than him, he would have no thoughts about her approaching him for financial gain. The truth, however, was that although Gladys did have an Aunt Mary who lived in Honolulu at one time, she was still very much alive at that time. And Aunt

Mary did not possess a fortune to the tune of three million dollars.

The other key element for Gladys and her plan was to demonstrate that she is available for the doctor. Sensing the real possibility that somehow W.D. and Leslie may encounter each other at some point, Gladys developed a strategy of defense. She informed W.D. that her husband, Leslie Merle Lincoln, had died in London during World War II, having been killed in an air raid. She also claimed that Leslie had a twin brother, an evil twin brother, named Lester Melvin Lincoln. They were so identical to each other the only way to differentiate one from the other was to find a birthmark at the hairline over the ear on the evil twin.

Once the twin brother learned of Gladys' impending inheritance of three million dollars from Aunt Mary, he had forced himself upon Gladys and tried to assume the identity of his brother Leslie. He had physically abused Gladys and was a real terror to her, and she claimed he was vicious, brutal, and a psychopath. Gladys was very frightened of Lester.

This information alarmed W.D. greatly, fanning his desire to protect Gladys in any way he could do so. W.D. returned home to Caldwell at the end of February, and they continued to correspond via mail.

Gladys and her plans seemed to be accomplishing her goal. But in reality, what is her goal? Is it to find a husband, the love of her life? She has had five husbands so far and appears to be heading toward the sixth. And she has treated each husband very badly, resulting in brief marriages only. It does not appear that married bliss is really what Gladys is desperate to achieve. It is the chase, the realization that a man, a new man, an exciting man, is fighting for her attention, for her love. But the truth is that Gladys has no love to give. She is completely engulfed with her desires, her needs, her powerful hunger for attention. Gladys loves only Gladys, and her over-arching, compelling need is to have men attracted to her. Remember, she is only 13-years-old emotionally.

The truth of this realization can be seen that while married to Leslie and pursuing W.D., Gladys is simultaneously engaged in a relationship with another citizen of Sacramento, a Mr. Leo O'Shea. It is not known how serious this relationship has progressed at this time, but the mere fact that it exists is an indication of the depth of Gladys' need to have men dangling on the hook for her.

Leslie and Gladys' marriage continued to deteriorate and he filed for divorce on April 24, 1946, about a year and a half after his return to his home and his wife. The listed cause on the divorce petition: cruel treatment. However, Leslie felt remorse and truly wanted to do whatever he could to salvage his marriage to Gladys. Only 4 days after filing for divorce, on April 29th, they reconciled. At least, Leslie thought they did.

Three weeks later, on Saturday May 18th, Gladys left Sacramento to visit family in Reno. Leslie was not invited, and she traveled via Greyhound bus since she did not drive. It is not clear whether she didn't drive at all or whether she didn't drive due to her drug habit. On that same date, W.D. left Caldwell on a road trip, without advising Floyd and Lola of his destination. That destination was Reno, Nevada.

CHAPTER 6

The good doctor and Gladys met in Reno and checked into their hotel together. On Monday, May 20th, 1946, Gladys married her sixth husband. The day after their wedding W.D. celebrated his 51st birthday. This is a departure for Gladys from her previous marriages, now marrying a significantly older man. On the marriage application she stated her age as 35, but she is actually 39, and is only one month shy of 40 years old. She also said she had been married previously but that her husband was deceased. Of course, he is not deceased, and Gladys has now committed bigamy. However, who keeps track of such things? No one seemed to know, or to care.

The newlyweds spent a wonderful weekend together in Reno, reveling in wedded bliss. This was such a wonderful and thrilling time for W.D., as he had been without intimate female companionship since his divorce from his first wife in 1942. Never in his wildest dreams did he imagine that at this age he could attract such a beautiful young woman.

The couple agreed that in view of the problem of the evil twin brother they should keep their marriage a secret for the time being.

On Tuesday, W.D. returned to Idaho, first driving to St. Anthony to visit his sister Sarah.

Sarah was aghast. She could clearly see that her dear brother was totally mesmerized by his new wife, and Sarah had never seen him happier. This was very good, and she was pleased to see Willis finally look so happy and excited. At the same time, she had deep reservations about Gladys. Everything she heard convinced her more deeply that

Gladys was big trouble. She sounded like a gold digger, and Sarah doubted the story about three million dollars. She also sounded like a drug addict from W.D.'s description, and even Willis himself realized she had a problem with overdosing on her medications.

But how do you say something negative when your brother is so obviously thrilled and happy? What right do we have to rain on someone else's parade? How do we know our judgment is better than the man who is the center of all these sudden events? Just because Sarah had her grave doubts didn't mean she knew what was best for her brother. And Willis wanted Sarah's approval so much. Sarah concluded she had to mind her own business and keep her mouth shut, and do everything she could to support her "little brother" whom she had loved since his birth.

After visiting with Sarah, W.D. drove on home to his ranch and Floyd, Lola, and the children. The plan was that Broadhurst would come to Sacramento on about July 1st to get Gladys and her belongings and take her back to Idaho with him.

On Tuesday, Gladys also returned home. To Sacramento. To her husband. To a marriage that <u>he</u> was trying to save and <u>she</u> had torched.

The newlywed couple continued to correspond frequently, particularly the doctor who was head over heels in love. He also was quite worried about his new wife and her perceived danger from the evil twin brother. As soon as W.D. arrived home, he penned this letter:

```
Letterhead:Dr. W. D. BROADHURST
Drugless Physician
THE IDAHO FIRST NATIONAL BUILDING
CALDWELL, IDAHO


     Sat.
```

Dearest Wifie,

So happy to get my first letter from you on Thurs. as I was uneasy about your safety. While at sisters I had a dream & I told her that things weren't going so well with you & I'd bet you had had another mixup with that brute. However, while on the subject of sister did she ever write you? I told her all about us & our marriage & she said she was writing you. She was very happy to think we had gotten together but very sorry about your state of health & trouble. She is one mum sister.

The big roundup starts June 15th & I'll not be in or around Jordan until about July 1st, so hardly know how I'll stand not hearing a word from you, cause I am very much in love with my Dear little Momma. Did I ever tell you I love you? Nope, never heard the word, just caught your vibrations. Darn my Daddy he does love me

Honey did you get the hundred dollar P.O. money order? Hope so. Now I'll mail you another $200 today & I want you to get out of that town. I had thot you could go to Long Beach down to your cousin's for a time & surely you could find a room eventually there. Now pack what you have, leave no forwarding adds., buy your ticket part way & then re-buy another. By no means leave any clue as to your whereabouts & by no means have any correspondence to Sac. Why not Daddy? Nobody talks if they know nothing, &

no pressure can be brot to make them talk. Give them the slip until I can get some place for us to live. Better get out as soon as possible.

Now as to your bills for Dr. & etc., find out how much & see if they will be O.K. until I can get something sold, then I'll be able to meet them. Better get going immediately Honey as we need each other & no lunatic like that guy can stop us. Certainly wouldn't tell Pete or the Mrs. – **NOBODY**.

Now these are only my suggestions & not demands so do the best you think possible, but please Honey get away from there.

You can find good respectable Drs. to give you the shots & get away from all that fear which will mean a lot, besides a change in climatic conditions. As soon as I return I'll try to send you more money.

Honey Sweet, for gosh sake buy yourself some clothes as you certainly need not go around in tatters. Clothes certainly don't make the man, but they help the appearance a lot & you can be so darn cute when you really fix up. Naturally, I know how you feel, no pep & no ambition to do anything, but one can never allow themselves to drift into a no-care attitude cause just see how much we have to live for. Daddy loves you in tatters, but he is so proud of his little spick & span Mrs. also. What will you do for me? "Anything humanly possible, Dear." O.K., listen to husband.

Now I am just talking Honey & that is who is going to make our lives heavenly for I know you are of my very heart & soul - Talk things over, discuss everything & then do the best for the most concerned. Right? I do love you, your prince does.

Needless to say our first nite was heavenly & to think of the more heavenly things to come when you are well & all worries obliterated & peace reigns for us again. I'll do my best in every way possible to make you happy & I in turn will be happy too. Gosh I'll bet you tease me for some more - Candy.

Do not suppose I'll get another chance to write before I leave, but want you to get away as soon as possible. Change add. at P.O. & not allow any mail to go out to 2228 ½ H St. Should have been a detective. I wonder if I could get Sac. to deputize me this fall & I'll get that dirty Brute.

Must run so until later I am,
Your loving
Broady Husband

How long can a secret be kept hidden? He might have his theories about how to protect her and she might pretend everything is normal and try to act as usual, but the truth has a way of bubbling up to the top of the sludge pit.

The doctor wrote often and had encouraged his sister Sarah to write to his new wife also. Gladys did everything she could to intercept all these letters and hide them from Leslie, but in mid-June of 1946 Leslie got to the mail first, and found and opened two strange letters, one from a doctor in Idaho and the other apparently from his sister. That was the end of keeping the secret, and that was the final end to Leslie's love for Gladys and his desire to remain married. After a huge confrontation, the couple separated and Leslie scheduled an appointment with his attorney to add bigamy as an additional cause to the petition for divorce.

Gladys was in complete panic. She was afraid for her physical safety, and she was afraid Willis would be notified in some way of the fact of her bigamy, destroying all that she had been working to achieve. She had to get to Idaho to escape any further consequences of her duplicity. W.D. had just begun the summer roundup, moving cattle from the spring range onto the summer range, and had told her he wouldn't be available until after the 1st of July, but Gladys could not take the chance of waiting that long. Something had to be done, so she wrote a letter to Floyd.

Scribbled at top of letter: *Tell Broady to drive down as he will need the car.*

Sac. Calif
June 20/46

Dear Dr. Adams & Family:

Am most pleased to meet you if only by phone etc. Dr. Broady has told me so much about you folks I almost feel I know you already. Doc, I have a serious problem, I must get word to my husband, Dr. Broady at once, that I am seriously ill with blood poisoning in my left leg & before the decision is made to take off said foot I feel that my husband (Dr. Broady) should be here to say yes or no! I feel he would say no, but regardless Doc, please please contact Dr. Broady & tell him to come as quickly as he can. I know he is busy & on roundup, but if I die he wouldn't be able to stand it. We sincerely love each other. He & I only had three short days together. We were so happy. He has been sending me some money, but it's him I need. I just have a room here & the folks have asked me to move or at least have my husband come to my rescue. Have a brother in F.B.I. but they won't tell me where he is. I imagine overseas he is under gov. orders & isn't allowed to disclose his whereabouts.

Please scuse the scribble. I don't usually write so badly but I've had no food for 5 days & am in terrible pain – you can't buy butter, eggs, meat, bread & very few clothes. I surely never want to see Calif again. Did Dr. Broady tell you about my aunt Mary Ralphs Johnson who died last August in Honlulu T.H. She left Dr. & I nearly three million dollars plus my own departed parents estate now in probation. The Hawaiian estate will be thru Probation about 1st of the year, so you can see Broady need not work himself to death. Course I always want him to do the things which will make him happy. I know he enjoys the cattle. I do too but right now, you will have to make him see I need him at once. Otherwise I would not change any of his plans for the world, but I'm about to die doc, & am pleading with you to find Dr. Broady & inform him of the truth. I think he loves me enough to come to me in my desperate plight.

Broady knew I was thin & run down & I expect he wanted me to stay here till fall & take liver & B1 shots. Had built up late, but I stepped on a rusty nail & it didn't take much to undo all the building up process. I know you will do your best to tell him what has happened. – Tell him to drop everything & bring what summer clothes he has, my rent is paid here till July 15th. However the main issue is it's a matter of life or death with me. Dr. Engelberg was out this a.m. & dressed my leg. He said "You better get in touch with your husband, you aren't doing so good." I said I didn't know where he was, so will have to leave that up to you to find him & tell him to come.

I'm sorry I have to bother you, as Dr. B. had meant to keep his marriage a secret. He told sister Sarah Allen & she wrote me a lovely letter.

Please don't fail me
Love to All

Gladys Ralphs Broadhurst
2228 ½ H Street
Sacramento Calif

Phone 27452

P.S.

Sent letter & wire 19th. Travelers Aide sent wire today. I spent three years in Service too. Army nurse. Ist. Lt. never went overseas but they surely kepted us busy. Had all four brothers & myself in. My baby brother was killed & one lost in France. He was found alive but had amnesia due to head injury. Sterl the other brother was in plane crash, & is in vets hospital in L.A. Jess my eldest brother is Capt. in F.B.I. So we know there was a war as we were all in it. I don't think Sterl will ever be able to walk much as his legs are still in casts. The air mail letter I sent Broady is very important because it contains our marriage certificate. I tried to keep it a secret but he wrote me as Gladys Ralphs Broadhurst & sister Sarah same so most everyone I know here knows. It wasn't because either he or I were ashamed, just that he had no house & he wanted to wait till Fall. The rest I'll leave to you Dr. Adams. Please.

Love,
Gladys

As can be imagined, Gladys' letter caused a huge reaction in Caldwell, Idaho. There were a dozen issues and two dozen questions created by this letter. The doc had married? Secretly? Without telling his nephew and business partner? Who is this woman? Is this for real? She sounds a little crazy with all the things she is claiming in the letter? Is she really sick and dying? How could W.D. have married this woman without telling anyone? Where are W.D. and his new wife going to live? Does this mean Floyd and Lola and their children need to move out and find a place to live? What about the medical practice? Have W.D.'s plans for passing it on to Floyd changed? Why did W.D. keep it a secret? Is this all a hoax? What about the three million dollars? That seemed too outrageous to be true also. But there are people in this world with that kind of money. Is this all true?

Floyd and Lola talked about the letter for an hour, first deciding it was all false, then thinking it was too fantastic to be anything but real. Then they weren't so sure.

There really was only one proper response to this letter. Floyd drove to Jordan Valley to the ranch, then since there was daylight left, rode on horseback to the site of the roundup, where he found the doctor turned cowboy with his crew. Taking him aside, Floyd handed the letter to the doctor and waited anxiously for the response.

No response was needed. The look of alarm on W.D.'s face as he read the letter let Floyd know the letter was indeed legitimate. W.D. finished the letter and handed it back to Floyd. "We have to go. Give me 10 minutes to get things in order here and we'll ride back to the ranch tonight. I'll head for California first thing in the morning."

W.D. told Floyd the whole story as they rode back to the ranch.

"Listen, Uncle Willis, I want you to know that Lola and I understand the Caldwell ranch is your home, and we absolutely would never want to intrude on your life. As long as you were single, we thought living with you would be good for all of us. I know how much you love the children. But now that you are married, I know you want to live there with your new wife."

"No, Floyd," W.D. replied, "I never intended for you to move out. That house is just as much yours now than it is mine. I would like for you to continue living there, as long as you want. But Gladys and I may have to live with you for a few months until I get a new place for us to live. Is that OK with you?"

"OK? Of course it is OK, Uncle Willis. We would be delighted to have you and your new wife stay at the house as long as you wish. It is plenty roomy enough for all of us, so please do not feel any pressure to make a decision fast on that score. And we are thrilled at the chance to meet your wife. She sounds like she is having a tough time, and perhaps she and Lola can hit it off and help each other out."

Early the next morning, June 23, 1946, W.D. left the Jordan Valley ranch and drove to Sacramento, a 9- or 10-hour drive, if you don't make many stops. Fortunately, the doctor had a nice, well-kept 1941 2-door Chevrolet Deluxe 5 passenger coupe, of which he was very proud. It had the famous "Blue Flame" engine that provided 85 horsepower. It was very comfortable and reliable and he was able to make good time. Arriving late in the afternoon, he went straight to 2228 ½ H Street where he found his new wife looking terrible and loaded her and her personal belongings into the car, then drove to a hotel on the other side of town. They spent the night in the hotel, hoping to avoid any possible confrontation with the evil twin brother, Lester.

W.D. was extremely alarmed at the condition of his wife. She was groggy and listless, and did not look at all healthy. Her speech was somewhat slurred and she slept almost constantly. W.D. was concerned about the medication she was taking and suggested she should cut back. Gladys was adamant that she needed the Nembutal to help her, so he didn't push it. He concluded they should stay another day or two in the hotel so she could recuperate. Gladys did seem to improve some, but W.D. knew he needed to get her back home to Idaho where Floyd could assist him in deciding the best course of treatment for Gladys.

When asked about Gladys' condition after her arrival in Caldwell, Floyd later testified "Well, she was in bed and she was apparently awfully drowsy, I will use the word "real" drowsy, in fact she was almost unable to be aroused from this sort of drowsiness."

After Gladys was put to bed and both doctors had an opportunity to examine her, they had a serious discussion between themselves about how to proceed. After considering various possible steps to take, W.D. said, "if Gladys is to die, and we are chiropractors, the people would resent that," so he decided they should ask Dr. Thomas Mangum to come down the next day and examine her, for that purpose.

After his examination and asking lots of questions, Dr. Mangum sat down with W.D. and Floyd and stated Gladys was in very bad shape. "She is addicted to this sleeping drug Nembutal, which among addicts is called 'goof balls,' and we've got to admit her to the hospital and wean her from this drug. Nembutal, also known as pentobarbital, is used as a sleep aid, sedative, and has a number of other uses. However, it can be fatal if overdosed or taken with alcohol. It has been used for euthanasia and executions to end life for both humans and animals. This is very serious, and failure to take action could result in her death."

As soon as Dr. Mangum departed, W.D. got her up and dressed and he and Floyd helped her to the car, and she was taken to the hospital in Nampa and admitted. Gladys kept asking for Nembutal in the hospital, but they tried to switch her to something else that would satisfy and somewhat gradually get her off the Nembutal.

The close supervision and treatment given Gladys by the hospital were very successful. Within two weeks she and the doctor packed and left Caldwell for the Jordan Valley ranch to begin the haying season. Haying season is a good time for everyone, and it was very good for Gladys. The fresh air and the camaraderie with the hay crew were very helpful in getting her spirits restored. Being an attractive and gregarious woman endeared her to all the crew. There were six men on the crew. Some were old guys, like Ben Mills who was 65 years old, some middle-aged ranch hands like

Jack Gallagher who was 35, and others were boys barely in their twenties like Alvin Williams. But young and old alike were quite taken by Gladys. And when she played the old piano and sang to them, all the men were enthralled.

Eastern Oregon is beautiful country in its own austere way. A great deal of the country is sagebrush and challenging. These areas are home to jack rabbits, antelope, sage hens and quail. You can travel mile after mile and it all looks the same, punctuated by the occasional gulley or dry creek that only has water for a brief while after a rainstorm.

Water is king. If you have water rights, you can irrigate and till the land and have bountiful crops. Eastern Oregon and Southern Idaho are famous for their corn, potatoes, alfalfa, mint, hops, and many other such products.

Without water, you have more sagebrush. The lawyers in this country feed their families on the fees they earn representing farmers who sue for water rights. My grandfather, P. J. Gallagher was just such a lawyer, and he helped establish the laws and precedents that constitute water rights laws in eastern Oregon as they stand today, both in the cases he tried and in his service as a member of the state House of Representatives.

During the haying, W.D. and Gladys slept in an upstairs bedroom until it got to be too hot, then they moved into a tent out in the yard under a tree. The crew slept in the bunkhouse. It was a very pleasant time filled with hard work during the day, a delicious supper they all ate together at the same table, and enjoyable evenings. It was pleasant until the inevitable happened.

Sheriff A.A. Moline of Canyon County, Idaho, had received a request to serve process of an amended divorce complaint by Leslie M. Lincoln vs. Gladys Ralphs Lincoln, which added bigamy as an additional cause for the divorce petition by Mr. Lincoln. The sheriff tried to serve these documents after W.D. and Gladys had left for Jordan Valley, so he was never able to successfully serve the amended complaint. However, word reached Gladys that the sheriff had asked for her, and she came to the startling realization that her marriage and her plan for the doctor were on the verge of collapse. If the good doctor ever found out Gladys was still married to Leslie when she married W.D., everything was doomed. Swift action was essential.

CHAPTER 7

When faced with a crisis, some of us panic and make sudden and often disastrous decisions. Others become paralyzed with fear and struggle coming up with any semblance of how to move forward. But there are some people who always seem to come up with a plan, to find a way to respond to the crisis. They don't always make the best decisions, but their logic usually leads them down a reasonable path. And sometimes they come up with ideas that are brilliant. We may not confer brilliance upon Gladys, but we have to admit she was creative.

In order to prevent Willis from learning of her bigamy via her being served by a law officer in Idaho, she decided her next step needed to be to return to California to settle the divorce process and calm things down. It was a great idea, but a little tricky in the performance. First, Gladys did not drive. Second, she couldn't have W.D. do the driving, as then she wouldn't be free to take the steps that were needed. Third, she needed a plausible excuse for the trip to California. But she managed to pull it all together, as usual.

On Friday, August 2nd, Gladys told W.D. she needed to return to California to take care of some business; business necessary to finalizing the estate of Aunt Mary and eventually receiving the three-million-dollar inheritance. The doctor said they were very busy at the ranch, but he could take two or three days to drive to Sacramento and return, in order for her to take care of her business. His wife told him there was no way that was long enough, that due to the complexity of the estate it would take more like ten days to get everything

'TIL DEATH DO US...' | 47

done. "No," he said, "there is no way I can be gone from the ranch that long, this time of year. There is just too much to be done."

W.D. was puzzled and hurt over his wife's decision to go to California, but he agreed to give Gladys the use of his automobile and have someone else drive her on the trip.

After much discussion, they agreed that Gladys could be gone 10 days, no more than two weeks, and that they would find someone to be her chauffeur. Gladys suggested Ben Mills, but the doctor said he was too old and not that good of a driver. She then suggested Jack Gallagher, and W.D. at first agreed. After thinking about it later, he realized he wasn't comfortable having Gladys spend 10 days with a strange man on such a trip. It wasn't that he didn't trust his wife, he said to her, but people would talk about it and the gossip could be ugly. Gladys replied that she "didn't give a damn what the people of the community thought, so long as she had a clear conscience." But then it turned out that Jack had left the area and they could not find him.

They finally settled on Alvin Williams as the chauffeur. He was just a young kid and no one would have any such thoughts about his wife and this young man. W.D. told Bernard that Alvin was selected because he didn't have anything else to do, and he knew him well, and would trust him with his horse.

Alvin Williams was a polite young fellow, but not too worldly wise. His experiences were limited to the Treasure Valley area. Alvin's fondest dream in life was to be a cowboy. He always wore cowboy boots and a cowboy hat, and his jeans always had to be Levi's. Wranglers were for farmers.

When W.D. first broached the idea to Alvin, the young man wasn't too keen on the idea. The doctor asked Alvin how he would like to go to California.

"Well, I don't care a whole lot about it."

"You will be gone only about a week, possibly two weeks at the most," W.D. told him.

"Oh, I don't have very good clothes, and I really don't want to go down there," Alvin replied.

"Well, it won't take many clothes," Willis argued back.

"But I'm not a very good driver."

"Have you ever driven in Boise?" asked W.D. When Alvin replied "yes," the doctor went on, "That is good enough. You don't have to be a very good driver to go to California." W.D. was really trying hard to convince Alvin, as he seemed absolutely to be the best choice for this task.

Alvin still didn't agree to the plan, only that he would make up his mind. That afternoon the doctor's wife came out of the house while the hands were waiting for lunch, and she asked Alvin how he would like to go to California.

"I have planned to go to California sometime. I just don't know when."

That evening W.D. asked Alvin if he had made up his mind. He offered Alvin $5.00 per day plus expenses to go to California and reiterated they would be gone only a week or two. After asking his boss if he was positive it would only be a week or two, Alvin finally consented.

On Monday morning, August 5, 1946, Alvin and Gladys left for California in W.D.'s 1941 Chevrolet Deluxe coupe, and with some of his money.

PART II - PERSUASION

CHAPTER 8

Alvin Williams and Gladys Broadhurst departed the Jordan Valley ranch for California, making it to Reno the first day. When they arrived, Gladys suggested they go to dinner and the theater for a movie. That sounded like a good idea to Alvin, but after they emerged from the theater, it was pretty late. So, Gladys said there wasn't much point in paying for a hotel, so why not just drive out into the country outside of town and sleep in the back seat of the car. They had blankets and pillows, so they could be warm and comfortable.

Alvin wasn't so sure about sleeping in the car with the boss' wife, but he was quite enamored by her, and anything she wanted was going to be just fine with him. After they snuggled in comfortably, they talked for a while. Gladys told Alvin that he sure looked an awful lot like her brother Bud. She asked if she could give him a "brotherly kiss" on the cheek. Later, while on the witness stand, Alvin was asked by the District Attorney what effect that kiss had on him. His reply, "That didn't have much effect, but the next one did." Her next kiss was on the lips, and when Alvin was asked how that affected him, he replied "That's something I can't tell you - I don't know how to explain it."

In the morning they drove on to Truckee, California, where Gladys' brother Sterling, whom they called Tony, owned a campground known as the Big Chief Auto Camp. They were assigned to different accommodations (Alvin a cabin, Gladys a pup tent), but during the night Gladys came to Alvin's cabin asking him to get some things from the car. After he helped her carry her things to the tent, she then told him she was afraid to sleep alone and asked him to sleep with her in her bed. Alvin agreed, arising early in the morning at 4:00 or 5:00 AM to return to his cabin.

From that time, they slept in the same bed every night for the whole trip.

Gladys and Tony both began calling Alvin "Bud," because he looked so much like their brother who had died 18 months earlier from wounds sustained in WWII serving in Italy. The travelers stayed ten days at the Big Chief Auto Camp. It was now their scheduled time to return to Idaho, but Gladys had done nothing towards achieving her accomplished purpose for the trip. She had, however, had a wonderful time so far!

```
Postmark dated: Aug 7, 1946 – Boise,
Idaho and also Aug. 8, 1946 –
Truckee Cal (Registered)
Addressed to: Mrs. Gladys
Broadhurst, c/o Big Chief Lodge,
Sterling Ralphs, Truckee, CA

Registered Mail

Hotel Owyhee
C. F. MANN, MANAGER
Boise, Idaho

Wed. a.m.

My Dearest Beloved Wifie:

     Have I ever told you I love you?
Well here goes, as I am madly in love
with you & miss you more than anything
in the world. Thot it bad enuf to be
away from you for a few hours, but now
days & weeks creep into the picture
it is terrible. Hardly know how to
tell you how much I miss you & love
```

you but a little imagination will get very close to the answer.

Disked two days & came down last nite - rose early yesterday 4 a.m., & went to work cause I didn't have any Momma in bed with me. Came in for breakfast about 6:30 & then ate no lunch as I wanted to finish.

Dr. & Lola feeling much better & had a nice talk with them about things in general. Lola stated her actions were caused from her being sick & not from any unkind feeling toward us as she loved us both very much. I feel certain that they got my point of view & know exactly how we feel about the whole setup.

George Vogt, our neighbor next door north had a birthday last nite & since they had a loudspeaker & yard all lighted we listened to the program from the steps of home enjoyed it very much. **Mommie I love you.**

Today I came to Boise to bring some side boards to uncle Billie, list the stock ranch, see Mr. Cranston, the Grocery Dept. & incidentally obtain a birth certificate. Guess I was never born for they have no record earlier than 1911. Was I born or was I just kidded into this old world? Anyway I have the form to fill out to be sent to Mrs. Adams for an affidavit & then I'll know if I were born.

Honey I am enclosing $100 bill for you & since I left the add. on the box am taking a big chance on you getting this. However, I'll register it so I'll be certain that it does not go astray.

If only I could hold you in my arms & tell you I love you for just a moment how happy I should be. Not long until I do I hope. I am so terribly lonesome & then Bernard being gone next week will make it worse. Gosh such a silly Daddy.

Have on my light trousers, green silk shirt & blue famous brands tie – already for the rodeo tonite. Wish my darling were here to be with cause we could have so much fun.

Hope you are getting along fine & that you know I am thinking about you every second & loving you so much.

To be hearing real soon & to be seeing you sooner, I am

Your most loving

Dr. Husband

(Written on the side of the last page): Think I'll go to Jordan tomorrow.

Gladys wrote to the good doctor at about the same time:

Postmark: Truckee, CA 8/8/46

Big Chief, Cal

Darling, Darling, Darling,

I miss you, I love you. How much is as the vastness of the blue blue sky here. Forgive me honey please for not wanting you to come at this time, it's so beautiful here, it hurts one's eyes. Al is overwhelmed. He's speechless. He wants to stay here. He is opening shingles for Tony. He drove very well, but it was so hot we nearly died. Will come back in the night. We got a parking ticket at Reno, one peso. Never did find out why??

I go to court Monday 10th - going before another judge - would have gone yesterday, but Tony is ill. Has been working too hard. We played together the other night & really had a time so spect he is tired. He was so happy to see me he cried. He looks fine tho, but stomach is haywire. Needs a course with my daddy. They were amazed how good I looked. Had my hair fixed nice at Reno, & so mommie just looked her best for her brother.

How I appreciate you darling. I know how hard it was to let me go, but soon we can go together always.

Don't work too hard darling. I miss you at nite always snuggling up to my honey - it's cold here and no daddy.

Will write again tomorrow Darling. Helping Gwynie today. Help is short. Write me here precious. I love you, I adore you, my darling dearest man in the world.

Love from us all
Your lil mommie wife

Big Chief Camp
Box 625
Truckee, Calif

Gladys was a little off on her dates, as the 10th of August in 1946 was a Saturday, not a Monday. However, W.D. did not seem to notice. He was much more interested in her professions of sweet love for her husband. Little did he know that she was engrossed in a full-fledged affair with her cowboy lover at the same time she was writing these terms of endearment.

Another letter arrived for Gladys from W.D. while she was still in Truckee. It gives us a much better insight into the thinking of the doctor while she was away from him on this trip:

```
8/15/1946

Envelope postmarked from Jordan
Valley, Aug. 15, 1946
Via Air Mail

From: Dr. W. D. Broadhurst
Jordan Valley, Oregon
To:Gladys Broadhurst
c/o Big Chief Camp
Box 625
Truckee, Calif

Thursday 15 - 46

My Darling Dearest Mommie:

     So happy to get your second letter
today & sorry you had not received
any of mine. However, one was written
Wed. after you left enclosing a $100
P.O. money order, which I know you
rec'd cause I rec'd the return card.
Needless to say it was rec'd by Mrs.
S. A. Ralphs Aug. 12. Now another was
written Thursday and another last
```

Sunday so you should have rec'd all by now. A card was sent to Sac. The same date of the money order. Now how is that? However, to date you should have rec'd three more than I have rec'd.

Terribly **MAD** & if you were here, so I could prove it to you, I would take it all out in giving you one of the greatest lovings of all times. Such a Momma with everything Daddy loves & yet all I can do is hope, pray & imagine how I should love to have you in my arms to pet & love you as we both love so much. No Darling I have no thot of anger & if you do not receive letters as often as you should like, remember the many things to be done during the course of the day, especially being alone.

Have all the ground ready for fall barley, one & ½ days of riding, one day fixing a gate just east of the house, cemented posts & really hung it in grand style. While speaking of riding rode the Cow Creek country yesterday & found four of our cattle.

Today I went to Caldwell to get gasoline, weed spray & more primarily to get a check on how the cattle sold at the O.K. sales yard. Not bad but I was offered more here for the steers than they were selling for at the yards. May sell about 50 soon. O.K.?

Darling I never worry about our little misunderstandings & only look at them as a means of a greater understanding. While a child we use to have a list of ditches on the farm

& I was quite the irrigator & quite often a dam would wear out & from that break it taught me that the next had to be stronger & so a greater understanding. So it is with our little misinterpretations – just a means of knowing our likes & dislikes.

Naturally everybody has had past experiences & so the history, character & reputations of us all are made – some good & some bad, but all in all I feel we rate above the average in building a reputable history of our lives. I married you for better or for worse, & with a full knowledge that I loved you for what you are & whatever you have or have done in the past, I question not & that is none of my business, for it is the YOU of today I love & it shall always be so. We voluntarily tell the things we want to & resent having histories pried open & made a public book. In all the peoples I have dealt with this is a self evident axiom. True today & always will be.

Of all my experiences with women I would not trade one of your sweet, sweet smiles & kind words for all all of them. Fine women to be certain, but it is My Momma that grappled my heart 20 yrs ago & still has it as spellbound as the cat & the mouse. So worry not My Dear One for a heart given so completely as mine will not change as nite the day but only as the great doer of things decides it is time to part. Mommie I love you so much my heart really aches for you.

To be alone without you is the most difficult thing I have endured since I parted 20 yrs. ago from you. I know you love me dearly & will soon be home but somehow I just cannot understand why you aren't around to be kissed, loved & ready to go to bed. Gosh Momma, how long must this go on?

Going to ride the range tomorrow & Sat. Jack Staples & I are going to spray morning glory on both places his & ours. We use the big cattle spray & haul it around in the pickup. Have two 30 ft. hoses with vapor like nozzles. Guess you have never seen it - it's a honey for grubs & lice. Have a lot of weeds down home so may go down as soon as Bernard gets home.

Have partially figured the food bill & as near as I can figure it, it cost $1.00 per meal per man or $3.00 per day for each man. Fay charged me $6.00 per day. Very expensive I should say.

Have found so many eggs that I have the pantry cluttered, yet we had to buy eggs for haymen. No justice in giving HANDS things to do unless they are guided in the right way. Thank God it has been a quiet week.

Happy to know of the expected arrival & hope all is O.K. with them. Never worry about her working as that is as necessary as food. Just avoid undue strains & all will be O.K. The finest COLTS I have ever seen born & with the greatest ease are the ones where their mothers worked. A homely comparison, but a fact.

Glad Jess is home & I hope for
good but I guess no such luck.
     Give my kindest regards to all &
tell them that if I do not die from
the loneliness I'll be seeing them
sometime. Bed time so My Darling I
love you, miss you & need you every
moment.

Your lonesome Daddy

Human nature is actually a fairly predictable force in our lives. Even when we think we are unique and different than the average person, in truth most of us react the same and act the same. When we are opposed, we fight back. When we are loved, we love back. There is something intrinsically wrong with a person who is loved and does not respond with love, or at least appreciation. Because this is so "normal," it is particularly noteworthy when someone does not conform to this pattern. Gladys certainly did not. How could she read such a fine letter with such fine intentions, and turn and go to bed with another man, not her husband? What kind of person does that?

Gladys and Alvin left Truckee and drove on farther south in California, where they checked into the Hotel Padre in Bakersfield, registering as "Mr. Al Williams and Wife". The next day they continued on to Taft, where she checked on some items she had in storage, spending 3 or 4 hours in Taft. Then they proceeded on to the coast and stayed in a lodge at the coast as husband and wife.

Gladys wasn't really surprised that Alvin wanted to spend every night in bed together making love. She knew men very well, and after all Alvin was only 23 years old. A young man like Alvin has tons of energy and insatiable desires! But being 40 years old now, almost twice Alvin's age, Gladys needed a break. Her solution was to insist that Alvin take her to a movie, which idea appealed to him also, as he was fond of movies. They went to dinner, then caught the movie playing at the small theater in town. The movie currently playing was "The Postman Always Rings Twice." If movies had a profound effect on Gladys and her psyche, this one was destined to greatly impact not only her but also Alvin and the doctor and all those who knew them for the rest of their lives.

"The Postman Always Rings Twice" is a dark film about a drifter, Frank Chambers who gets a job working at a gas station/diner for a man named Nick Smith. Nick has a much younger and very beautiful wife named Cora, played by Lana Turner. Frank and Cora fall in love and engage in a torrid affair, and ultimately decide they must kill Nick in order to have a life together. This they do. Despite their careful planning, the ending of course does not turn out well for either Cora or Frank.

Gladys is enthralled by the movie, and her first comment to Alvin after they get in the car to return to the lodge is, "Gee, it's too bad something like that can't happen to the doctor!"

She wasn't joking.

Gladys meant every word of it when she told Alvin that it would be great if the doctor was killed. Whether she had that thought earlier is a big question. Was that something she had in mind when she first contacted W.D. to re-establish their relationship? Did the idea come to her after she had married the doctor and moved with him to Idaho? Was it because of her new relationship with Alvin on the trip? Or had the idea just come to her as she sat in the dark theater and watched the story play out on the screen? We will never know for sure, but we can form a pretty good supposition.

The paramours then headed back north and finally made it to Sacramento on August 19th. They drove around Sacramento as she pointed out the sights to Alvin, then directed him to her brother Gene's place. Gladys was quite proud to show off Alvin, who was tall, strong and handsome.

He wore a black Stetson hat, cowboy boots, black trousers and a black western shirt with white trim on the pockets and seams, all new and provided to him by Gladys courtesy of W.D.'s money. Alvin considered himself quite the man of the west. The couple enjoyed a good visit with Gene, who went by "Red," and his wife Elsie.

Afterwards, the lovebirds checked into and registered as "Williams, Al & Mrs.," at the fashionable Senator Hotel in Sacramento, which was where Gladys had first seduced W.D. only seven months earlier. The irony was not lost on her, and she hid a small smile at the realization. This hotel was a significant cog in the wheel of her plans.

The Senator Hotel was also the scene of quite a bit of drama over the next few days.

That night, as they prepared for bed, Gladys began to work on Alvin to persuade him to kill her husband. Special District Attorney Blaine Hallock related in his opening statement:

"The testimony will disclose how the defendant first merely hinted that if the doctor could be done away with, she and Williams would be rich and they could live happily together and life would be sweet indeed."

Alvin was not at all keen on the idea, and he said so. The problem was that Gladys had Alvin completely spellbound and her persuasive powers were in full gear. The prosecutor described him as "impressionable, young and easily swayed." That was a true statement. Alvin was way over his head in this war of wills, and he had no chance.

During their discussion about the idea of killing the doctor, Alvin tried his best to avoid making that decision. However, Gladys was way ahead of him.

Gladys used all her tools in swaying Alvin to her thinking, not the least of which was her body. She was a very attractive woman and she was a mature, experienced woman at the art of making love. There is considerable debate, however, whether Gladys only engaged Alvin as her pawn to achieve her goal of killing the doctor, or whether she truly loved Alvin. A strong argument could be made that Gladys at the very least was very fond of him. She seemed to really enjoy their time together, and they engaged in many activities that she loved. Perhaps it was because she really didn't seem to have matured beyond her teenaged years. Gladys and Alvin went to movies, danced, partied and had a thoroughly wonderful time together. She developed a handful of pet names for Alvin, calling him "Al" or "Man Friday" or "Allen."

Another tactic used by Gladys took the discussion into the spiritual realm. Alvin, who later testified that he had never been to Sunday school and had only been to church a few times, knew very little about the Bible or religious beliefs. He had, however, heard of the Ten Commandments. Gladys reminded him that they were guilty of violating the 7th commandment, "Thou shalt not commit adultery." He knew what adultery was, and he was enjoying it immensely. She went on to say the 6th commandment is "Thou shalt not kill." Gladys told Alvin she had been a minister of the Gospel, and she knew all about spiritual things, and that if anyone is guilty of violating any one of the Ten Commandments, then he is no worse off for violating any of the other commandments. Murder was no worse than if you would go out and steal an apple. She also said, "Besides, Doctor Broadhurst is more animal than he is a man." So, he might as well not worry about any consequences for the act she was encouraging him to perform.

Gladys eventually won Alvin to her way of thinking that the doctor must be "eliminated." What put him over the edge was her claim that W.D. mistreated her and had beaten her several times. There is no evidence of the truth of that, and in fact everything points to the doctor's love and indeed infatuation with his wife. But it was enough to overcome Alvin's resistance to her plan. Now their discussions centered on how to carry out the deed. Whenever they were alone, that was all they talked about. It is no simple thing to decide to murder someone and come up with all the details of what should be done, how it should be done, when it can be done, and where it should be done.

It is not enough to plan a murder; one needs also to think about how to avoid being caught for it!

All their planning was interrupted, however, by a little issue of husband number 5. Somehow Leslie had learned that Gladys was back in Sacramento and where she was staying, and he called the hotel to try to speak to her to arrange a meeting to talk about their marriage, and their divorce. Gladys agreed to meet him in the lobby of the hotel, so she and Alvin went down to wait for him. When he arrived, Gladys introduced Alvin to Mr. Lincoln, then she asked for him to wait somewhere else, so Alvin headed for the bar.

After Lincoln left, Gladys told Alvin that this was the evil twin brother she had told him about. She told him again how her husband had died in the war overseas and this evil twin brother of his was trying to take on the identity of his dead brother, in order to steal her inheritance. The brothers were so identical even Gladys had a hard time distinguishing them, the only way to know for sure was to find the small birthmark above the ear on the evil twin. Gladys also told Alvin this twin brother had threatened her several times and had beaten her up.

The meeting between Gladys and Leslie Lincoln was highly unsatisfactory. It was very clear that this marriage was over, and now all that was left was the legal proceedings. Which meant those amended divorce papers needed to be served on Gladys. Lincoln's next stop was at the office of his attorney, Irvin Ford, and together they went to meet with a private investigator named Joseph Kral, to engage him to serve Gladys with the amended divorce complaint.

Leslie and Kral returned to the hotel, but were unsuccessful in finding Gladys there. But Leslie had a pretty good idea where to check next, so they headed over to Red's place, that is, her brother Gene's. When it turned out Gladys wasn't there, Kral took Leslie back to work then decided to go back to Red's place and wait and watch for a while. His patience paid off, because at about 3:30 PM he saw a Chevrolet coupe with Idaho license plate 2C 140 pull up in the alley and a man and a woman went inside. He went to the front door and questioned a man who gave misleading information.

After a little more waiting, Kral observed the car in the alley being driven around to the front. A man got out, looked around and motioned with his arm, then a woman scurried out and jumped in. Kral followed them, lost them, found them, then forced them over and jumped out of his car and ran to the other car. Alvin tried to act the tough guy and shouted that Kral had no right to make them pull over. Kral stared at him and told him to "shut up," and Alvin said no more.

Gladys denied being Mrs. Lincoln, saying she was Mrs. Broadhurst and the driver was Mr. Broadhurst. Kral just grinned and handed her the papers anyway.

As Alvin sped away, Gladys threw the complaint out of the car window.

However, the next day Gladys did go to her attorney's office, Mr. D. D. DeCoe. DeCoe filed an answer to the complaint for Gladys, which allowed the case to go to decree, thus ending the risk from this source for giving W.D. the information that Gladys was still married to Leslie Lincoln at the time she married the doctor.

This accomplished Gladys' real reason for coming to California. She could have returned to Idaho then, but she didn't. It has now been two weeks since their departure, and the two lovebirds could have returned from their trip, mission accomplished. However, they spend another four weeks in California, ultimately spending a total of seven weeks less one day on this trip that was supposed to last a week or two.

Why is Gladys acting like this? Is it her intention to inflict as much pain and anguish as she can on her husband? Is she just being a child and finding it impossible to tear herself away from all the fun she is having? Has she fallen in love with Alvin to the extent that she just can't bear to return to Idaho where she won't be able to carry on with him like she is doing now?

Postmark: Truckee, CA 8/27/46

Big Chief
Truckee

Darling Daddy Dearest:

Why haven't we received answers to our wires dear? - Jess, Tony & Red, sent wire asking you to come at least for a few days. I wired you twice, once here and once in Sac. Please darling you need to get away for awhile & it's so gorgeous here. Then Jess may go back soon & we want to have a family party before he leaves. May not see him again. Would you darling? I know it hurt you beyond words when I left, but I just had to fight this out alone - I love you, adore you honey & I'm only asking one thing more. Please come for a few days. We are so happy you are a part of us now & there will never be another time so ideal for all of us to be together - I know you are busy, busy but a few days in this spot will take away all your cares. Alvin is wild about it here and wants to stay & cut trees. He has been very nice to me. I'm glad you chose him as he is honest & decent. He is going to ride for Big Chief Camp Sept. 2nd in Rodeo. Please come honey. Take the bus & then Mommie & Daddy can go home together.

Have taken care of all I could for the present. Will tell you all about it.

Thanks for your letter and the $100.00 you are so good to me. I love you!

I'm fine cept I'm awfully lonesome. I'd never wanted to be away again, but honey I did the thing I wanted & I'm free of fear on that score. Had you helped me, I'd still be weak. Please come & see your surprise. Honey don't fail me. It's about the most important thing in my life to have you meet my family & spend a few days with us. I just can't bear it if you don't come. Please daddy - Sweetheart.

Called Dr. Adams and the only wire you got was the one from Sac. You didn't get the one from the Ralphs Brothers inviting you down. I feel Jess must leave soon so hurry honey. Take the Bus & then call Big Chief Camp & we will get you at Truckee.

Bye darling, please don't fail me
—

Your loving wife
Flea X O

Send whatever you feel like in money, but won't stay here much longer but would so love a few days with you here. It's an ideal place for a few days honeymoon.

X O X O

CHAPTER 9

The couple has now been gone for 4 weeks.

Whose actions are harder to fathom, those of Gladys or W.D.'s response to them? What kind of woman plots the murder of her husband then begs him to come spend time with her and her family? How can she write about Alvin in such glowing terms to her husband, knowing how unhappy he has to be that she is spending weeks with the young man? Why does she keep talking about this present she is getting for W.D. when in fact no such present exists or will exist? The only "present" she has in mind is an early grave.

But the doctor's actions are almost as inexplicable as his wife's. Who would allow his new wife to go on a weeks' long road trip with another man? What kind of man is W.D. that he harbors deep jealousy and resentment yet wills himself to put that all aside and expect the best out of a woman who is anything but stable and dependable?

Willis did come down via bus from Caldwell to Big Chief Auto Camp in Truckee, and they all went to the rodeo in Cal Pine. Alvin became a contestant in the bareback riding contest and took top honors, winning 30 dollars. Gladys was very proud of her cowboy hero.

The doctor wasn't. He and Alvin had a serious conversation while they were together in Truckee.

"Doctor, this is beautiful country down here. I wouldn't mind staying here in Truckee and working for a while. Tony and Gwynn are great people, and I'm really enjoying it here."

"Well," W.D. replied, "that is very good, because I can't afford to pay you any longer to chauffeur my wife around, and if you are going to stay here, then Mrs. Broadhurst can stay a while longer and when I get ready to come back I will take her back home with me then."

The doctor wrote a check to Alvin for payment in full for Alvin's wages as chauffeur for Gladys. The next day they drove W.D. to Truckee where he boarded a bus for his return trip home.

What happened? Didn't Gladys tell her husband that if he came down to the Big Chief Auto Camp, he could drive the car back to Idaho and she would go with him? Didn't she write, "Take the bus & then Mommie & Daddy can go home together?" And now he is leaving . . . alone. Gladys is staying behind; Alvin is staying behind. The doctor's car is staying behind.

And what about the "surprise?" What was it? Didn't Gladys write "Please come & see your surprise?" So, what was it? Did she have a surprise for him? Any surprise? He would certainly have been surprised to learn of Gladys and Alvin's sleeping arrangements when he wasn't there, but it is doubtful that is the surprise she had in mind. The good doctor went away very sad and perplexed.

Postmark dated: Sept, 7, 1946 - 9 AM
- Winnemucca, Nev.
Addressed to: Gladys Broadhurst, c/o
Big Chief Camp, Box 625, Truckee,
Calif.

Hotel Humboldt
Gus Knezevich, Managing Owner
Winnemucca, Nevada

8 P.M.

My Most Darling Wifie:

Needless to say I left the most important part of this old framework in Big Chief, & altho you may not be able to locate it in houses, tents, cars, rivers & etc. it should be ever present in every movement, act, or thot you think. Possibly not visible to the naked eye, the ears, or the skin, but it is there & in such an abundance that I feel completely lost - possibly I'll recover but slowly. Momma Dear, to me, you are the grandest, dearest, most Divine soul I have ever known. Believe me Dearest, this is as I have always felt, & trust you are as completely sold to our vastness of love as I.

Only as you have peace of mind can I ever hope to, for whatever disturbs you likewise effects me. I can be brave & shout to the hilltops that it doesn't, but I am only kidding the inner man & soon Mr. Conscious gets on the scene & utters in silence, "Man know thyself better, for two hearts that have loved, longed & bleed for each other so long can never be troubled unless both are effected in like manner." Darling this is true as nite the day & rightly so for vibrations travel & are received by those who are in tune to receive them & I know that I am one who is a perfect receiving set for your vibrations.

All I have ever said or done has always been with the greatest feeling & spirit of trying to help you. Wrong in many things & subject to errors & mistakes always but when convinced of these facts, I can admit it frankly & in no way ever feel an unkindly feeling or thot toward My Dearest. Only as we can do these things can life be worth the living. I love you.

I have known ever since I met you in Feb. that you were ever so troubled & in my humble way have given the best I have. Possibly not always to your liking, but I am only human & have many human weaknesses, but in my SOUL I have every thot of trying to be helpful. That which I do not see & do will be the things & reasons why I could do no more. My heart is still there just the same.

I have my chin up & feet flatly on the floor & can look the whole world in the face & tell them that I love you adore you & worship the very earth around you. I can offer no more & likewise no less, as this completes the cycle that I would do nothing knowingly to detract from that kindred sacredness. And as surely as the sun rises & I see its lite, I am always willing to give you everything in life that my capabilities permit. They may not be all the glamour & fame that some possess, but they will be genuine & as rich as my very life can make them.

Often we are misled by blarney, glittering brightness & our emotions & think how foolish we were to accept anything other than the above mentioned, but still deeper far deeper than the eye can see or the ear hear lies a brilliance that has depth, breadth & a sense of endurance that lasts forever. So it is in my love for you, & I believe with your love as well, it will last until the end of time.

If our time to part should come tomorrow, I could truthfully say that as far as I had known how to help you, I had not failed. However, not knowing many things have taken place, all for which I am truly sorry, but from these I can build & avoid the same mistakes again.

I can see now, after having talked to you & understanding some of your past how easily I could have been more of a hindrance than a help in your liberation of fear & many other troubles. Yet My Dear, until I knew it was that big pioneering heart of your most ardent lover that spoke in challenge to anyone that attempted to harm you. Just my primitive nature protecting his loved one. Forgive Me Darling & forget any unpleasantness that may have come our way. As certainly as I know I hold no grievances or a thot in this wide, wide world other than that one that can be added to make our lives harmonious & beautiful.

Had you been well & without fear & worry, I often wonder, if life would have had more meaning and if thru these trying times the greatest understanding will not come. Never for a moment have I regretted our marriage, otherwise it has given me someone to try to help & I most assuredly hope & pray that my handicaps to you can be far offset by possibly a greater help. Anyway, I hope this is true, most fervently.

Now Darling give my regrets to G. & Tony for not bidding them goodbye this a.m. but I didn't see them & we had very little time to spare. Thank them a million times for their extreme kindness & assure them that in SHIRT & SOUL I love them as tho they were my own.

Leave this lonely town at eleven & arrive in Caldwell 6:25 a.m. Tired & lungs pretty tight but head seems to be draining quite well. Worry not for your Daddy wants to live just to love & help you all his life & I hope that be a long long one.

Momma Dear, I so hope that the continued stay with your folks will be happy, healthful & that when you decide to come home you will do so with a heart full of joy & a feeling & knowledge that your Daddy is lonesome, arms wide open & has a much broader knowledge of how you feel & why so. All I have is yours & I share it with you as freely as I share the greatest love in the world.

Darling I miss you so much & to love you & to know you are present is my life in its entirety.

Nite Darling & please write often to your very lonesome Daddy.

Most & all my love, Daddy.

Is there a normal woman anywhere who would not be thrilled to receive such a deep, heartfelt declaration of love and adoration as that penned by the lonely doctor while he waited for the time to board the bus for his lonely journey homeward, to his lonely home to await the return of the wife whose very presence he coveted so deeply? Willis was a very lonely man. Lola later testified, "After Dr. Broadhurst returned from California, he seemed very much upset and very worried and very heartbroken in fact."

But in California, Gladys and Alvin were having a great time! With the doctor gone, they could continue their nocturnal visits and daily enjoyments. Later when Alvin was on the witness stand, when asked if he was "pretty well satisfied" with what he was doing with the doctor's wife, Alvin replied, "Well, I wasn't complaining any."

Gladys replied to W.D.'s letter from Winnemucca on September 10th of 1946.

```
Postmark: Truckee, CA 9/10/46

Sunday

Darling:
     It was sweet of you to write
me the nice long letter from Winn.
Thanks.
     I am lonely without you - to hear
from you so soon is a pleasure - I
worried much as I knew your cold was
not too good. I also stayed in bed
Friday & Sat as my cold has sprouted
into quite an affair. Jess was up today
& took me for a brief ride. He surely
was surprised to see me & told me
would be happy too if I could remain
longer. You were a dear to let me
stay. I do feel piggy like about the
car, but am glad I can come home when
& as quickly as I get things straight
here. May have to make one trip to
```

Sacramento. I'm sorry your visit was so short & not too pleasant. I'd hoped you would have a really lovely time (Darn me, huh?) Next time be better.

Gwynn goes to the Dr. Thursday. She isn't doing right. I'm afraid she is going to have a miscarriage. Pat has two new infections & has hourly shots of penicillin. Some hospital we have here. Every one sick but it looks we are on the mend.

Do hope you will try not to worry too much or to be too lonely. Once I get this all done here I won't have to come back. Wow, it's been a most trying time.

Just got lunch. Gwynn's in bed so maybe I will close the joint for Luke.

It's been warmer darling, really hot to go out.

Honey dear, I'll write more tomorrow, my head aches so from sinuses, I scarcely can breathe.

I miss you,
Your loving Mommie

That was short and sweet, without her normal gushing pronouncements of love and adoration for the doctor. Perhaps it was because she was preoccupied with all her plans. Her plans for the doctor. Her plans to continue to work on Alvin to keep him engaged on their plans of murder. Plus, she had her wedding plans to think about. Wedding plans??

On Tuesday, September 17, 1946, Gladys and Alvin drove to Reno to get married. Alvin later testified that Gladys told him that since they were living as husband and wife, it would be very nice to go through a marriage ceremony. They obtained their marriage license right after lunch on that day, and were married at 3:00 PM. However, Gladys used the name "Elaine Hamilton" on her marriage license and Alvin used his real name. Gladys listed her age as 30, she is in fact 40 years old. Alvin listed his age as 28, but he is actually only 23 years old. Alvin wrote that he had been married previously and was divorced, but in fact this was his first marriage. Gladys stated she had been married previously and that her husband was deceased. Of course, he was not deceased. Not yet.

Gladys and Alvin have now been gone from Caldwell for six weeks. She finally decides it is time to head back, but not until first going to Sacramento one more time to meet with her attorney, D. D. DeCoe.

As they drove, they continued making their plans on how to dispose of the doctor.

Gladys asked Alvin, "Do you have any ideas of how the doctor could be disposed of?"

"No," he replied, "I don't. I don't have no definite ideas. However, he might become lost while we was hunting for cattle."

"Well, Alvin, if he did become lost, he would have to never be found. If the doctor was to ride for cattle, how are you going to get out in the hills in order for the Doctor to come up missing?"

"I might get a job riding for the doctor," Alvin suggested.

"Well, we have got to go through everything and check and re-check it," she answered.

Our new newlyweds finally made it back to the area where they had begun their journey, but instead of going to Caldwell they stopped in Ontario, Oregon which was only 35 miles short of her home, arriving at 11:00 PM on September 20th. The next day they visited Alvin's uncle and a cousin, then a friend. That evening they went to a dance in Homedale, staying out until 2:30 AM the next morning.

They then returned to the Carter Hotel in Ontario, again registering as "Mr. & Mrs. A. L. Williams."

On both nights at the Carter Hotel, they discussed the Doctor's demise. Alvin testified that they decided "if W.D. were to come up missing I could go on being the chauffeur for a certain length of time and after that length of time if he was not found he would be pronounced dead and all of the estate would automatically change over to her and then after that her and I was to get married, have a public marriage."

Having gone to bed so late, the couple slept in on Sunday, then they went to the Turf Club in Ontario for lunch. After eating, they headed to Wilder and watched a double feature movie in the theater, then drove around until dark. Finally, they headed for Jordan Valley, but no one was home at the ranch. After eating dinner at the bus depot in Jordan Valley, they returned to Idaho, and went to the Caldwell ranch, finally arriving home at 11:30 PM. Their journey has ended. They have been gone 7 weeks less a day.

CHAPTER 10

"Good morning, Alvin."

Alvin awakened to see Doctor Broadhurst standing over him. After they arrived at the Caldwell house that night, Alvin had spent the night in one of the downstairs bedrooms while Gladys had gone upstairs to sleep with her husband. One of her husbands.

"I'm very glad to see you have finally brought my wife home to me. How did you make out?"

"I made out just fine, Doctor." Then Alvin rolled over and went back to sleep.

W.D. returned to the breakfast table with Floyd and Lola, and shortly thereafter Gladys came down from the upstairs bedroom. Gladys walked up, kissed W.D. on the cheek and said, "I think I will go back to bed and wait for Man Friday, and eat breakfast with him, he is a little bashful." Lola couldn't help seeing the look of pain in the doctor's eyes.

W.D. left the house shortly after breakfast. Lola wanted to talk to Gladys more, but could not find her. She ultimately concluded that the doctor's wife must be in the bedroom where Alvin was sleeping. They both came out soon after and Gladys prepared breakfast for the two of them. Lola sat down with them and they related stories of some of their experiences in California on the trip and things they had seen. They acted very carefree and jovial and were having a good time together, laughing and talking. Later, after breakfast, Lola observed Gladys sitting on Alvin's lap while they talked together and laughed.

The doctor returned to the house about 10:30 that morning, and the demeanor of Gladys and Alvin changed abruptly. They did not speak to each other unless necessary and there was no more joking or laughing. When W.D. returned, he went to kiss Gladys who was playing the piano, but she turned her face away, so he just lightly kissed her on the cheek.

It turns out that W.D. had gone into town to the bank and had opened a joint account for Gladys and himself, depositing $1,000.00 into the account. This surprising move creates a litany of questions. Why did he do that? Is he totally clueless? Is he trying to buy back her love and loyalty?

One thing W.D. knew for sure, and that was he wanted Alvin out of there. Since he had already paid Alvin in full when he was at the Big Chief Camp, it was only a matter of taking him to town. W.D. and Gladys sat in the front seat with Alvin in back, and they took him into Caldwell where they dropped him off. Then the doctor drove around town and introduced his wife to his bankers, business associates, and friends. Alvin hitchhiked to his parents' house in Parma.

Good riddance. That was the last he would see of the little twerp. Or so the doctor thought.

This all took place on Monday. W.D. and Floyd were planning to leave on Friday with a group of friends on their annual elk hunting trip, which normally lasted about two weeks.

On Tuesday evening, Floyd, W.D., and Gladys are in the front room of the Caldwell house.

Gladys spoke up, ""Doctor, if you were to go hunting, or up on the range, and something was to happen to you, I wouldn't have sufficient money to bury you."

"Oh, I don't think you have anything to worry about. I'm going to be fine. I've got many years ahead of me in this old life."

But Gladys was insistent, almost hysterical in her feelings about the subject. With the doctor leaving in just a few days on the hunting trip, she was adamant that he needed to do the right thing to ensure her well-being in the event of some unforeseen catastrophe.

The next morning W.D. stopped in at his attorney's office and wrote a new will cutting off all other relatives and leaving everything "to my beloved wife Gladys Elaine Broadhurst". The will specifically stated, "I do not intend to give anything from my said estate to any of my brothers or sisters or to any of my other relatives. It is my desire that they shall receive nothing from my estate."

The District Attorney claimed in his opening statement that she pressured him to create this will.

Thursday was preparation and packing day for the hunting party, as they were leaving early Friday morning for the trip. Both doctors, W.D. and Floyd, were going on the trip, along with their usual group of hunting buddies. About 6:30 PM, the phone rang and Lola answered it. The caller was Alvin and he asked to speak with W.D. When the doctor came on the line, Alvin invited both him and Gladys to join him that evening going to a movie. When W.D. declined because he was still packing for the trip, Alvin asked to speak with Gladys. She walked into the hallway with the phone and spoke with Alvin out of the hearing of anyone else in the house.

"No, Alvin, we can't go to a movie tonight because everyone is still packing for the hunting trip. Why don't you come over tomorrow about noon, as everyone will be gone by then?"

Lola later testified that W.D. was very much disturbed that Alvin was calling his wife. He thought he had seen the last of Alvin and had not anticipated continued phone calls from the young man. However, he put those thoughts away from his mind, as he had so often done over the last seven weeks. "Out of your thoughts, out of your worries," he said to himself as he went about finishing packing his gear for the hunting trip.

The hunting party left at 6:00 AM Friday morning, and Alvin showed up about noon complaining of a bad cold. Lola didn't think he looked all that sick, but Gladys immediately took charge and began to minister to the poor sick boy. She insisted that Alvin go to bed, and put him in W.D.'s bed. She took his temperature, then gave him a sponge bath and a pair of W.D.'s pajamas to wear. For the entire two weeks the doctor was gone, Alvin slept in W.D.'s bed and Gladys occupied the adjoining bedroom. The two bedrooms were side-by-side with a window between them that could be opened. This window was normally kept shut, but Gladys left the window open during these two weeks. After a few days, the furniture in the bedrooms was rearranged so that the headboards of each bed were up against the wall, under the window. With the window open you could reach over and touch the person sleeping in the other bed, and with only a little effort you could just crawl through the window onto the bed in the other room.

Lola was beside herself, and didn't know what to do. Deep down in her heart, she was convinced that Gladys was the most evil, the most manipulative person she had ever met. Lola was appalled at the demeaning, disrespectful way Gladys treated her kind relative. Lola was truly fond of W.D., which made her want to do anything she could to help and protect him from this woman.

But it was just for this very reason that Lola felt compelled to do anything she could to have a good relationship with Gladys. She later testified, "I intended not to let anything that had happened stand in the way of my friendship with Gladys; that I was going to be very friendly with her; and how she had hurt Doctor by being away and not explaining why she was away was none of my affair, and I was determined not to let it interfere with our friendship at all; that I wanted to be friends with her."

In her conversations with Gladys, Lola came to expect some pretty bizarre discussions. At one point, Gladys confided in Lola that "she hated men, and sex, and didn't know why she had ever gotten married again."

That is an amazing statement from a woman who has now married a total of seven men! But for some strange reason this attitude did not seem to extend to Alvin. When Lola commented about him, Gladys replied she "wouldn't trade a hair of his head for any other man she had ever known." Was she being truthful when she said that? Or was this all a part of her conspiracy? It seems that for whatever reason, Gladys truly did not include Alvin in her list of men she hated.

During another discussion, Gladys asked Lola if she had ever seen the movie she and Alvin had seen together called "Leave Her to Heaven," a movie about a woman who had taken the life of her brother-in-law and her unborn child. She asked Lola if for any reason she ever felt she could take the life of another person. This was a very disturbing conversation to Lola.

Earlier, Lola and Floyd had also had numerous conversations about Gladys and her strange behavior. Lola told Floyd about the things she had observed about Gladys, and they discussed how they should handle this; specifically, what they should tell W.D., if anything. They ultimately came to the conclusion they should keep quiet. It didn't seem possible the doctor could be unaware of the things they were seeing. If he chose to ignore those things, that was because he wanted to do so. They reasoned that to force W.D. to acknowledge and deal with these issues would only cause pain, and probably would accomplish nothing. They needed to exercise discretion. Prudence was their byword.

Therefore, Lola settled into the role of watcher and chronicler. They might not speak to W.D. about his new wife now in an effort to not destroy his happiness, but the day may come when he would be very interested to know what has been going on, and Lola was going to have some information for him then.

Beginning on the first day after the doctor and his friends left for hunting, Gladys began working in earnest on Alvin to determine what would be their best plan for disposing of her husband.

Gladys: "Do you know where Sellway Falls is, Alvin"

Alvin: "No, I don't rightly know where it is. I know it is way up north. I heard Floyd and the others talking about their route, and they mentioned driving through McCall all the way up to Kooskia, then heading east."

Gladys: "Do you think you could go up there and find them and dispose of the doctor somehow? You would have to make it look like an accident, of course."

Alvin: "Well, I have no way to get there."

Gladys: "You could take the coupe."

Alvin: "No, I don't want to take the coupe. It would be too obvious that I was the one that did it."

Gladys: "You know, we need to buy you a car, a cheap car, something you could dispose of after this is all over."

Alvin: "Well, that's a good idea. I'll look for something that would be good for this."

Lola continued her careful observation of Gladys and her cowboy. At one point she saw Gladys go into the room with Alvin, then a while later emerged from the room wearing a different set of clothing. Each day, Gladys & Alvin would get out of bed and have breakfast together after Lola's family was up and done. Day after day, Gladys & Alvin left in the morning and returned in the evening in W.D.'s vehicle.

At one point, Lola had complained of cold feet and Gladys gave her electric pad to Lola, and Lola had asked to make sure Gladys didn't need it. Alvin responded to that, saying "she has so many covers on her bed now I can hardly turn over."

Gladys & Alvin discussed the murder scenario whenever they were alone. They discussed thoroughly the details about destroying evidence. They abandoned the plan for Sellway Falls and came up with the idea of waylaying the Doctor en route between ranches, where Alvin would hit him over the head then shoot him.

First, they drove to Jordan Valley and got a gun, but it was a .25-.35 and they couldn't find any shells for it. Then they went to Parma and picked up Alvin's shotgun and a bedroll at his house, that is, at his parents' house where he lived.

During the two-week period the hunting party was away, Alvin and Gladys and Lola went out several times. On the first Wednesday, they had drinks at the Morocco Club in Nampa, dinner at the Old Mill in Boise, then to the Circle Club, then drinks at the Rendezvous Club in Boise. Then on Saturday, the three of them went to a dance in Homedale.

The three went to movies on two occasions and also two more nights of dancing at various clubs in the area. Gladys and Alvin were intent on having as good a time as possible, and Lola was very interested in going with them and watching their interactions. At one point in one of the clubs, Lola left the table to use the ladies' room, and as she walked away, she saw in a mirror that Alvin reached over and kissed Gladys, thinking he was unobserved.

When she was on the witness stand, Lola was asked why she went with Alvin and Gladys when they went dancing and drinking. She testified, "Well, I went out with her because she was the doctor's wife and because we had -- I was trying to make her think that I considered her as that because Doctor Broadhurst had asked me to do everything in my power to make her feel at home and make her feel welcome."

On October 2nd, the divorce trial between Leslie Merle Lincoln and Gladys Ralphs Lincoln was conducted in Sacramento, CA. Gladys did not attend in person, but was represented by her attorney Darold D. DeCoe. An interlocutory decree of divorce was granted, which was to become final a year later, on October 1, 1947.

The lovers continued to work on their plan to murder her husband. Alvin told Gladys, "I don't know if I could go through with it or not. I couldn't stand the sight of human blood." She asked him if whiskey would help him, and he said it would help settle his nerves. So, Gladys obtained a liquor license in Caldwell and purchased two quarts of whiskey to bolster his will power.

Meanwhile, Gladys and Alvin continued working on the idea of purchasing a cheap automobile he could use. They shopped around the country for an automobile to purchase. They looked in Boise, Caldwell, Nampa, and surrounding towns. Finally, they found and purchased a Model A Ford coupe for $200, which contained some left-over tools, including a big heavy crescent wrench. The seller was a young man named Winthrop Godfrey.

The couple decided that W.D. was to be killed by the wrench, but if necessary, the shotgun would be used to finish the job.

They also discussed what to do if they came under suspicion. They concluded they would mention Mr. Lincoln, as Gladys said he had threatened to kill the doctor.

Their final conversation was that Gladys told him he was to waylay the doctor on the road to Jordan Valley. He was to stick close to the ranch so that as quick as she found out when he was going, she could let Alvin know so he could be there when W.D. got there.

Gladys also went to the office of the H. J. Sloan Realty Company in Ontario and met with Mr. Edwin D. White, the realtor W.D. had engaged to sell his stock ranch at Jordan Valley, comprised of 2,000 acres of Delamar ranch and 600 acres of cliff side. She stated she had been sent by the doctor to find out how they were coming on the sale. She said they would rather sell it on a contract rather than cash as they had ample money and if they got the cash, they wouldn't know what to do with it.

Gladys told E.D. White she and the doctor met at Burley, Idaho and that they were quite intimate at that time, but, unfortunately she became acquainted with another man and they off and got married; and then along came the second world war and that she was a nurse all during the war, that her husband was killed in the second world war, and from her continuous nursing during the war period it broke down her health and she had been in California taking a rest and trying to recuperate.

The hunters returned on Friday, October 11th at 5:30 PM. However, W.D. refused to sleep with Gladys because the sheets were soiled, choosing to sleep on the couch in the front room. Floyd later testified that W.D. "seemed to be very much disturbed of the fact that Williams was at the house on our return."

The next morning at breakfast, W.D. said to Lola, "I understand that you have visited a few night clubs in our absence." Lola replied, "Yes, we have, that's right." He said, "Well, my wife wouldn't tell me a thing about where she had been or what she had done." Lola replied, "That's funny, because I told my husband every place we have been and everything we have done."

But Lola did not tell W.D. about the disturbing things she had witnessed during his absence on the hunting trip, "because Dr. Broadhurst asked me to do everything I could to make her happy, and he was trying so hard to make a success of his marriage; and I certainly didn't want to be the one to shatter his last hope."

After breakfast, Lola told Gladys she had told her husband every place they had gone and what they had done, and she was much disturbed. She said, "Will you ever learn that there are things which are best left unsaid, especially to your husband?"

That evening W.D., Gladys, Floyd, Lola, & Alvin went to a dance together at Homedale. W.D. didn't want to go, he was very tired and nearly ill. Gladys insisted he go, saying if he didn't, she was going without him, with Alvin. At the dance, W.D. said he was going to Jordan Valley on Sunday or Monday. Floyd testified he thought W.D. "seemed happy, very happy, he seemed to be enjoying himself at the dance."

Sunday morning, W.D. dressed and prepared to leave the house. Gladys ran from the bedroom, through the front room and past Lola into the kitchen, and she said "Where are you going? What do you mean by just coming in and kissing me, and not telling me where you were going?"

W.D. replied, "There is nothing to be so excited about; I am just going over to the neighbors."

Gladys replied, "I thought sure you were going to Jordan Valley without telling me." Then a few moments later she told Lola, "I don't believe I will ever understand him. I thought he was going to Jordan Valley without telling me, and I wouldn't have been particularly surprised."

That afternoon, W.D., Gladys, & Alvin went shopping for a travel trailer. The doctor cannot seem to shake Alvin! Alvin was like a lap dog that his wife insisted on keeping around, despite her husband's obvious displeasure over the situation.

The purpose of the trailer was because W.D. had a prospective buyer for the Jordan Valley ranch, and he wanted to buy the trailer and go on an extended trip through Arizona as soon as the place sold. He wanted to go on a belated honeymoon with Gladys. He said they were going to take their honeymoon in it — he was going to make up to his wife for their delayed honeymoon. He was trying so desperately to get his wife's attention back.

After they returned home, W.D. announced that he was going to Jordan Valley the next morning.

CHAPTER 11

As soon as she could get a minute alone with Alvin, she gave the news to him. Gladys' parting words were: "Get out there. Be there when he gets there, and for God's sake don't miss."

Alvin left that night at 11:30 PM, with his bedroll, 2 quarts of whiskey, a satchel of clothing, the wrench, and the shotgun. They said he was leaving for Nevada.

Alvin drove to the junction of the I-O-N Highway and Succor Creek Road, 14 miles north of Jordan Valley. This was wide-open sagebrush country and the highway does not have much traffic. Alvin pulled over and waited for daylight, sleeping in the car. He had the whiskey to help him keep warm on a chilly October night, plus his bedroll. When dawn came, he raised the hood of his Model A.

The good doctor did not cooperate very well with the conspirators, however. He didn't get up bright and early and head out as Gladys had imagined. He puttered around the house, then finally left in the early afternoon with his pickup truck, his horse trailer, and his pinto horse, "Rex." Even then, he didn't drive straight to Jordan Valley, but stopped off in Marsing. W.D. ate lunch at Smith's Restaurant in Marsing with Clarence Mullinix, a local stockman, spending a couple hours visiting with his friend. W.D. engaged Mullinix to come up to the ranch and help him count his cattle. When Clarence agreed, W.D. offered to give him a ride, but the stockman thought it best to get his car out of the shop where they were winterizing it, so it wouldn't get shoved out onto the street. They agreed Clarence would join the doctor the next day, Wednesday at the latest.

Meanwhile, Alvin is sitting on the side of the road, waiting for Willis to show up. Although there is not a lot of traffic on that highway, there is some traffic. And while Alvin waited, a local rancher named Joseph Fenwick and his hand, Clifford Dickson, drove by on their way to burn some sagebrush on Fenwick's property. They came by at 8:00 AM and saw Alvin parked there, but didn't pay any attention to him. They came back on their way to lunch at 11:45 and saw Alvin still sitting on the side of the road. After lunch, Fenwick went into Caldwell for some shopping and Dickson returned to the brush burning. Seeing Alvin for the third time, he stopped and asked Alvin if he needed any help. Alvin replied that he had car trouble and his buddy had gone to town to get some replacement parts. Clifford noticed that the driver of the car wore a white cowboy hat and a rodeo shirt with white trim around the pockets and cuffs. Seeing that he couldn't provide any aid, Clifford went on with his work.

However, Clifford did later testify that he heard a gunshot about 20 minutes before four PM.

Alvin's plans made with Gladys were not shaping up at all well. Not only has the doctor not shown up, but now Alvin has been clearly seen waiting for hours at the location where he plans to commit murder. All reason suggests that this mission needs to be aborted. Alvin didn't really want to do this anyway, and now it is going upside down. But he still hears her in his head.

"Don't fail me! Don't fail me! If you do, for God's sake don't come back!"

Meanwhile, Gladys is not having a good day either. She laid in bed until about 3 PM, at which time she called Lola in to tell her she was ill and staying in bed per W.D.'s instructions. She also said W.D. had had an argument with Red Wells and she was afraid Red would do the doctor harm.

Gladys also asked Lola to leave the front door unlocked, as Alvin might come by later and she wanted him to be able to come in. When Floyd & Lola returned that night about 10 PM, Lola mentioned Gladys' request, but Floyd made sure the door was locked.

Finally, at approximately 3:30 PM, the doctor's pickup came into view. W.D. started to go by Alvin, but Alvin waved at him.

Alvin testified, "He pulled up a little ways past me, stopped and got out and asked me if I was having car trouble. I told him yes, the gas line was clogged up on my car, and I asked him if he had a pair of pliers."

"He said yes, he went back and got the pliers and he came up to the car and handed me the pliers and I started to loosen the connection on the gas pipe."

"Well, I was excited and nervous and I was shaking quite a bit, and he took the pliers and started to disconnect the gas pipe; and I had the wrench in my hand, the big wrench, and I was supposed to lure him to the car."

"I stood by the side of him and I looked up the road, and I looked back the other way, and there was nobody around, and I started to hit him and I tried to quit then, and I seemed to hear a voice saying 'Don't fail me! Don't fail me! If you do, for God's sake don't come back' - and I hit him."

"He had hold of the pliers, and he dropped the pliers, throwed his hand to his head and held onto his head with both hands, and he kind of staggered around and he asked what hit him, he says, 'What hit me, Al?'"

"I says, 'I don't know, Doc.' And I went over - I made up my mind I was going to get out of there just as quick as I could, and I went and got my shirt out of my car and I folded it up and handed it to him, and told him to hold that on his head, maybe that would stop the flow of blood."

"And he was standing on the edge of the road and a car, a truck or car coming might - and I asked him to step off the road there, a car might hit him. He kind of walked around off from in front of the car. He stepped out on the old road, standing kind of in the middle of the old road, and I put the hood down on my car and I picked up the wrench, carried it around, started to get in the car."

"I had just put the wrench in my car, and I heard him move, he had been standing out in front of the car a little ways, and I looked around and he said, 'God damn you, I am going to kill you,' and he had his jackknife, and I grabbed - I reached in the car and grabbed my shotgun and it was loaded, and I pulled it out of the car, I just swung around - the gun was right by my side - I hollered, 'Don't, Doc,' and he didn't stop."

"I couldn't get away from him. I was standing right against the car, and I shot. Doctor dropped his knife and grabbed at his chest. I turned and started back the other way, and he went out - he got about halfway to the pickup and he fell, he fell on the road. And I looked up and there was a truck coming down the road, some truck that had a load of baled hay. I went out and grabbed Doctor and drug him off the side of the road."

"I pulled him off the side of the car and I throwed a blanket over him and got down between him and the vision of the truck driver - pretended to be working on the front wheel - and after the truck went by, I moved Doctor out into the edge of the sagebrush, then I picked up the knife that he had dropped, and hat, and put them in the car. Then I got in Doctor's car, in the pickup, and drove it up over the hill and took the horse out of the trailer, rode him back part way , then I left the horse; there was some tall sagebrush there and I didn't want to tie the horse up so he couldn't get loose, so I just wrapped the reins around the brush, then I rode back - I walked back from where I left the horse, down to where the car was, where I had left my car. I got in the car and I drove up to Shayville and I got some gas and I got some soda pop, then I drove on past Bill Harris' - or Joe Harris' - I couldn't be sure what the first name was. After I got past

Harris' place, I turned off on a branch that led from the oil over to the old Shayville road."

"When I got over there, I hid the gun, then I parked the car and I stayed there in the car until dark. As soon as it got dark, I drove back, tried to pick him up. I wrapped him up in my bedroll - rolled him up in my bedroll, then I got down by the side of him and tried to lift him up on my knee so I could get him on my shoulder so I could put him in the back of the car, and I got him up on my knee, and I stopped to rest there and he was awfully heavy, and I started to go up with him and I got overbalanced and I fell over backwards, and - well, all I could think of was just to get that body moved before somebody came along. I crawled under the body, after I got under the body, I rolled over and got his body on my shoulders, and I raised myself up on my hands and knees, and there was a fence right there close by. I crawled up on that fence post until I got up on my feet, and I started to walk to the car and I tripped and I dropped him."

"He fell on his head. Then I decided maybe I could back the car down in the barrow pit and that would make the back end low enough so I could put him in the car. So I left the car in the barrow pit, I took the lid off the trunk and then I took the spare tire off, and that left the back of the car about two foot and a half from the ground, and that way I managed to put the body in the back end of the car. Then I drove back, came back this way, came back to the Cow Creek Hill, up there, and I turned off the road at the top of the hill and I hid the body, then I took - I got two keys off his body and them two titles to the car, and there was a receipt from Mr. Billy Maher, showing that the doctor had paid Bill Maher a down payment on the ranch. I think there was somewhere around $135 in the billfold, and I took all that stuff and went back to the Caldwell ranch. On the road back, I stopped at Marsing; I stopped there and ate supper and I drove right on out to the Broadhurst ranch. After I got out to the ranch, I knocked on Mrs. Broadhurst's bedroom window. She got up and unlocked the door for me, and when I got in, I told her that I had done it, and I told her that I hadn't destroyed the evidence yet, but she says, 'Thank God! Go and destroy the evidence and then come back as quick as you can.'"

I'm quite sure God didn't have anything to do with it. This act was purely from Satan, and it is difficult to imagine how two people could consider this act, plan its execution, and then carry forward to murder an innocent man whose only fault was to love a woman who hated men.

And we have Alvin, who has compassion on a horse and removes him from the doctor's horse trailer and ties him to some sagebrush, because he cares about the welfare of the horse if he is left locked up in the trailer. Too bad he didn't feel more compassion for the man than for the horse.

Dr. Willis David Broadhurst was murdered just under five months after marrying Gladys and three weeks plus one day after Gladys and Alvin returned from their seven-week joy ride in California. He was murdered three days after his return from his elk hunting trip with his nephew and friends. His murder was planned by the wife he adored and carried out by the young man he had tried to help.

PART III -INVESTIGATION

CHAPTER 12

"Oh man, there is always some screaming emergency just as lunch time hits," the affable sheriff muttered as he reached for the ringing phone. Despite 22 years as the Malheur County Sheriff and the many intrusions into his personal life, Charles Glenn of Vale, Oregon loved his work. Most cases in this rural county dealt with fairly minor crimes from horse theft to drunk and disorderly. Today, Tuesday October 15, 1946, would be different.

It was unusual first because the caller was a doctor from Idaho. "Not my jurisdiction," Glenn thought. But he sat up and paid more attention when Dr. Floyd Adams related how his uncle's horse and truck and trailer had been found near Jordan Valley with no sign of the owner. This was no petty theft, this smelled different from the start.

Sheriff Glenn's first move was to contact Sergeant Walter Walker of the Oregon State Police in Ontario, then he and his Deputy John Koopman drove to Cairo Junction where they met up with Walker and another officer. They all piled into Glenn's cruiser at Nyssa and proceeded together to Shayville, a wide spot in the road towards Jordan Valley. Meeting up with Dr. Adams they continued on and drove off the main highway onto a dirt road, coming up to the pickup and empty horse trailer.

As Sheriff of Malheur County for 22 years, he judged he had run into about most situations a lawman would encounter in his career. He had plans to spend his last couple years in law enforcement passing on his experiences to Koop and the rest of the young deputies he had been grooming to carry on after his retirement. That was something he looked forward to immensely.

Oh, how wrong a man can be! Never in his life had he encountered such pure evil as he was about to find.

"OK, doctor, please bring me up-to-date on what you know."

Floyd began, "Dr. Willis Broadhurst is my uncle, and he owns a dairy farm just outside of Caldwell and a ranch near Jordan Valley. He left yesterday about mid-day to drive from Caldwell to the ranch in Oregon, but he never arrived. Last night about 9:00 PM, a friend of ours, Lionel Krall, who is the fire chief in Caldwell, came upon W.D.'s horse, Rex, running loose along the road. LC, as we know him, had ridden Rex numerous times and recognized him immediately as Doctor Broadhurst's horse. He took the horse on to Mendel Falen's ranch and they went looking for my uncle."

"The two went to W.D.'s Jordan Valley ranch, but he was not there. So, they went to the hotel in Jordan Valley to use their phone and called our house. My family and I live in the same house in Caldwell as Doctor Broadhurst and his wife Gladys. Krall spoke with Gladys and she told him the doctor had headed for the Jordan Valley ranch, so they knew something was wrong. They searched the area and after quite a bit of searching they found W.D.'s pickup and horse trailer. There was no one there, so Falen got in to see if the engine would start, thinking perhaps Doctor Broadhurst had engine trouble, but it started up just fine."

"The two, Krall and Falen, then went back to the Jordan Valley ranch to see if the doctor had shown up, but no one had seen him. Now everyone was deeply concerned about the welfare of W.D., so they got more help and continued searching. They tried again to call the Caldwell ranch late last night, but did not reach us. I guess we were all too sound asleep to hear the phone."

"These good folks searched through the night last night and found where the horse had been tied for some time, but that is all they could find. They called us again this morning about 5:00 AM, and told us what they had found. They spoke with W.D.'s wife Gladys again and asked if anything had been heard of the doctor. She said 'no, there hadn't' and she asked them to be sure to let her know if they found anything. They told her they had found the pickup and trailer."

"After that, they organized a large search party both on foot and on horseback, and they are still searching out here right now, as you know. I finally realized we had better get the law involved in this, and that's why I called you just before noon this morning, Sheriff. Thank you and these other officers for coming out to help us."

"You are very welcome, of course," Sheriff Glenn replied. "This looks to be a very serious situation, and we all need to do everything we can to get to the bottom of it. Tell me more about your uncle and give me any other information that may prove helpful."

Floyd elaborated to the sheriff. "My uncle is a very successful doctor of chiropractic, as am I. He has been a huge influence in my life and it is because of him that I also am a chiropractor. I served in the Army in Puerto Rico and Trinidad until the war was over. My wife Lola and I and our two children moved to Caldwell last November, so I could take over my uncle's medical practice. W.D. was ready to retire, so it seemed good to both of us for me to move here and continue the work that he had begun."

"Doctor Broadhurst was married once before, but that ended in divorce about four years ago. He has been a bachelor since then, up until a few months ago. He and his new wife Gladys were married in May, I think it was. I hate to speak out of turn or say anything prejudicial, Sheriff, but I have to tell you that W.D.'s new wife is a very strange lady. We didn't even know he was planning to get married until after it was done, and his wife hasn't really been around us all that much since their marriage. But we, my wife Lola in particular, have observed some very odd behavior by Gladys, some of it we think is inappropriate."

This caught the Sheriff's attention. "What do you mean inappropriate, Doctor?"

"Well, she didn't move up here to be with her new husband until over a month after they got married. I know that's not inappropriate necessarily, but it is odd. Then after she had been here for only 4 or 5 weeks, she told W.D. she had to return to California for a couple weeks. The doctor hired a young cowboy named Alvin Williams to be her chauffeur, because she doesn't drive. In fact, she's been addicted to a sleeping medicine that makes it impossible for her to drive."

"This 'two-week' trip ended up lasting almost two months, and the doctor was beside himself with anxiety about his new wife. As you can imagine, he wasn't happy about his wife spending 7 weeks with another man, traveling around the country. And then when Alvin and Gladys returned, the inappropriate behavior really escalated. The doctor and I joined a group of friends on an elk hunting trip from September 27th that lasted until last Friday, and Gladys and Alvin were quite intimate with each other while we were gone. This was observed by my wife. I can only imagine how they acted toward each other while they were gone to California together."

Sheriff Glenn took this all in, then thanked the doctor for filling him in about Doctor Broadhurst. "Of course, inappropriate behavior isn't a crime, Doctor, but I will keep this in mind, and I will definitely be speaking with both Mrs. Broadhurst and this fellow Alvin soon."

"Thank you, Sheriff. What should we do with the pickup? The key is still in the ignition. Is it OK if I go ahead and drive it home?"

"Yes, to the Jordan Valley ranch, but keep it handy in case we need to look through it again."

After Floyd left with the pickup and trailer, the officers spoke with several of those who were standing around and had been helping with the search. Officer Walker was speaking with one of the searchers, and motioned for the sheriff to join them. "Sheriff Glenn, meet Clifford Dickson. He was working in this area yesterday and he has some interesting information."

"Yes, Sheriff," Clifford took up the narrative. "I came by this area four times yesterday going to work in some nearby fields, and three of those times I saw a young man in an old Model A automobile parked on the side of the road. Finally, on the third time going by, I stopped and asked him if he needed any help, and he said 'No' and that a friend was bringing him a part for his car. That's all that was said."

"Thank you, Mr. Dickson," replied the sheriff. "That may be useful information. Do you think you could identify this man if you saw him again?"

"I suppose so," Dickson replied.

Tuesday morning after Gladys hung up from the call from L.C. Krall telling her they had found the doctor's pickup and horse trailer, she went into an emotional tailspin. Lola testified that she "sobbed little whimpering cries" at the news, and became quite unsteady on her feet. Lola helped her into her room and put her to bed. She couldn't talk and she couldn't hear what Lola said to her. After breakfast, Lola went back to Gladys' room to see how she felt. Gladys didn't answer, she didn't pay any attention to Lola and she kept mumbling things that Lola couldn't understand. Finally, Lola gave up.

Floyd was a little less charitable. His take on it was that "she was forcing a cry." "She was trying to show emotion," he later testified. "She was trying to, and in the apparent picture that I have of that she was dopey or under an influence of a depressant."

Alvin wasn't in much better shape. Lola also testified that Alvin walked into the kitchen Tuesday morning looking white and haggard, very nervous and had bloodshot eyes.

He was shaking so violently he spilled a cup of coffee and could not light a cigarette.

After Dr. Adams and Lola departed, Gladys and Alvin discussed their next steps. "Are you going to be all right, Alvin?" she asked.

"Yes, but I'm worried they might recognize my car. A couple fellows passed me several times while I was waiting for the doctor to show up, and one even stopped to ask if I needed help. I'm afraid they might remember my car."

"What can we do to prevent the car being recognized?" Gladys asked.

"I could change the wheels on the car and they would be less apt to recognize it."

"Well, go ahead and get it done. Do you need some money?"

"Yes, I may need a little money," Alvin replied.

"Well, take what you need out of my purse," Gladys told him.

Taking forty dollars from her purse, Alvin drove to a used car lot and traded the 450 by 21-inch wheels and tires for 16-inch wheels and tires, paying the difference of the cost in cash. He then went to the hardware store in Caldwell and purchased two cans of black enameloid paint and a brush, then drove north of town and painted the car from blue to black. Finally, he took the turtle back (the lid for the trunk) to a dump and dumped it. After accomplishing these tasks, Alvin parked the car in Caldwell on Blaine Street beside the Methodist church, then hitchhiked out to the Caldwell ranch to let Gladys know all this had been completed.

Tuesday for Floyd and Lola was a day of action. With heavy hearts and fearing the worst, they made plans to help locate their beloved relative and friend. Lola stayed in the office and took care of business and advised all patients who had appointments for the next few days that a re-schedule was necessary.

Floyd spent the morning helping with the search, then went into Jordan Valley and made his call to the sheriff. Following his meeting with the sheriff and taking the pickup back to the ranch, Floyd returned to the search location. He and Rudolph Jestrabek worked together searching, and toward the end of the day they came upon a location where the ground and the brush had been disturbed. Searching closely, they found what appeared to be bloodstains on the highway. They took two rocks that had the stains on them and started driving towards Caldwell with the rocks, but then decided they ought to notify some authorities of their findings, so they turned and drove to Vale, to the sheriff's office. It was now 10:00 PM.

The sheriff called Dr. Tacke in Ontario to arrange an analysis of the stains on the rocks to determine if they were human blood. Unable to reach Dr. Tacke, he called Dr. Joe Beeman in Boise to see if he would be able to do the analysis. Receiving an affirmative response, the sheriff arranged for the doctor to wait for Floyd and Jestrabek, who immediately left for Boise.

Reaching Boise at about 1:00 in the morning of Wednesday the 16th, they gave the rocks to Dr. Beeman, who performed the tests and advised that the stains were indeed human blood. He also called Sheriff Glenn to let him know the results as well. Floyd and Rudolph next drove to Caldwell and advised Sheriff A. A. Moline about the facts of the case. After a call between the two sheriffs, a meeting was scheduled in Caldwell for the next morning. A few more calls were made, then Sheriff Glenn headed back to bed. Again.

"Man", he thought, "I've had a lot of short nights and sleepless nights, but these nights where you get about three snatches of brief sleep between phone calls are the worst. You never get rested."

Arising early Wednesday morning, Charles Glenn drove to Nyssa where he met his deputy, John Koopman and Sgt.

Walter Walker and Officer Richard O'Brien of the State Police. After eating a quick breakfast in Nyssa, the four continued on to Caldwell and arrived at the sheriff's office about 7:30 AM. They met with Sheriff Moline and his deputy, Dale Hale. Floyd was there with them also.

"Men, we aren't exactly certain what has happened here, but we believe this may be a homicide investigation. Furthermore, we aren't exactly certain whether this occurred in Idaho or in Oregon, it's so close to the state line. Therefore, we're all going to work together as a team to sort it all out, and once we have answers to those two questions, we'll know better how we wish to proceed. Now, Sheriff Glenn told me about a Model A Ford having been seen near the scene of the crime, and Dr. Adams has confirmed that Alvin recently purchased an old Model A vehicle. We have located a Model A here in town that may be of interest. Some of us will check out this vehicle while the rest can head straight out to the crime scene." Sheriff Moline was a competent law officer, and everyone was fine going along with his suggestion. However, Charles Glenn had a sneaking suspicion this was ultimately going to fall right squarely into his lap.

The two State Patrol officers headed for Shayville to join in the search. Sheriff Glenn and Deputies Koopman and Hale went down on the street in Caldwell and examined a 1929 Model A Ford coupe bearing Idaho license number 2C 310, which was parked on the street near the Methodist church. It was freshly painted black, so freshly that the paint was still sticky. The turtle back cover was missing and in the seat was a small canvas bag containing some clothing, a pair of spurs, a package of Bull Durham tobacco and a partly-filled bottle of whiskey. There was also a can of paint and a used paint brush in the car.

Sheriff Glenn and Deputy Koopman left for Shayville to join the search.

CHAPTER 13

After meeting with the Oregon officers Wednesday morning, Sheriff Moline headed out to the Caldwell home ranch where he found four or five men gathered, including Dr. Adams. Telling Floyd he wanted to speak with Dr. Broadhurst's wife, they went into the house where Floyd introduced them to each other.

"I am the Sheriff of Canyon County, Ma'am, and as such I am very anxious to help in locating your husband. I would like to offer my services to do whatever I can."

"Thank you, Sheriff," Gladys replied, "I would like to introduce you to Al Williams, my chauffeur and bodyguard."

"How do you do, young man?"

"Howdy, Sheriff," Alvin replied.

"I would like to speak with you outside, alone, Al. Shall we go outside?"

Once they were outside, the sheriff told Alvin he would like them to go together into town. He then arranged with Floyd to take Gladys to the scene of the "accident," since Alvin would not be available to act as her chauffeur at that time.

The sheriff took Alvin into town and drove to where the Model A Ford, license plate number 2C 310, was parked.

"That is my automobile," said Alvin.

After getting this confirmation on the car, Sheriff Moline returned Alvin to the ranch. There was no one there, so Alvin went inside where he found a note propped up on a bottle that read, "Dear Allen: Have gone with Doc and Lola. Here are the keys. Please bring the car — Gladys."

Alvin got in Dr. Broadhurst's Chevrolet coupe and headed for Jordan Valley. Sheriff Moline returned to his office in Caldwell and arranged for the Model A to be towed to the parking lot behind the sheriff's office.

There were a lot of people out in that sagebrush country when Charlie Glenn and his deputy arrived. That's just the way it was in 1946 — folks helped each other when there was a crisis. It's still a lot like that today in Eastern Oregon. It is good country with good folks. When the two lawmen arrived, there were quite a few cars parked at the site, and folks were scouring the country on foot and on horseback as they searched for the doctor. Of course, there was no way of being certain that a body was out there somewhere, but all the facts pointed to the likelihood that something foul had happened to him.

"Let's find Walter or Dick and see what has been learned," Glenn suggested. Officer Dick O'Brien was easy to find, as he was sitting in his cruiser with Alvin seated beside him having a conversation. Sgt. Walker was standing around the fire with a group of men who were warming their hands and bodies from the cold. Sheriff Glenn motioned to him and they stepped aside so they could converse privately together.

"I've been here since about 9:30. The doctor's wife pulled in around 10:00 in the car driven by Dr. Adams. Dr. Adams also brought his wife and a child along with them. Mr. Williams arrived about 15 minutes after they did, driving that cream-colored Chevrolet coupe, which belongs to Dr. Broadhurst. He's a funny kid, and nervous as a cat. I'm considering him a very suspicious character."

"Have you any evidence that ties him to anything?" asked the Sheriff.

"No, nothing yet. It's just my guts talking to me," Sgt. Walker said.

"Well, I've learned long ago to trust your guts, Walter," smiled Glenn.

"While we're talking gut feelings, Charlie, I'm having similar feelings about the doctor's wife. If the young cowboy is strange, she is twice as strange. There's something about that woman that gives me chills down my spine."

"Well," said the sheriff, "the nephew and his wife have told me about the same. They don't have a very high opinion of her."

"Don't forget that the nephew or his wife could be a suspect too," chimed in Deputy Koopman.

"Yes, of course, John," replied Walker, "but they pass the smell test much better than the wife and our young cowboy."

At that, they walked back to the car where Alvin and Officer O'Brien were still sitting and talking. Shortly after they arrived, Gladys walked up and spoke to them.

"I would like for Alvin to drive me over to the Jordan Valley ranch, if you don't mind," she said. "I need to get a warmer coat and some of my personal items from there."

"I'm sorry, ma'am, but we need to talk to Alvin," replied Sgt. Walker. "He can't leave just now, but we'll be happy to help you out. This is Officer Dick O'Brien. Dick, would you mind giving Mrs. Broadhurst a lift?"

Realizing Alvin was under suspicion, Gladys showed emotion for the first time. She now began making alibis for him. "You know, Alvin was with me the whole day October 14th. He couldn't have done it because he is fearful of the sight of blood. There was a time down in California where a bus driver had been critically wounded and they brought him to this place where we were and I was taking care of him, and he was bleeding quite badly and Mr. Williams had fainted and I had to take care of him too."

"Not only that, he really isn't strong enough. The doctor is a much larger, stronger man than Al."

"If you think something really bad has happened to my husband, surely it must have something to do with my deceased husband's evil twin brother. You see, my previous husband was killed in London during World War II. He has an evil twin brother who is trying to take his place because I have an inheritance coming of three million dollars, and he is trying to cheat me out of it. He must have come here and done something horrible to my dear husband Willis."

"Also, there's another man named Red Wells who had an argument with my husband just a few days before he left. I don't know what it was all about, but this Red Wells was pretty angry and made some threats toward the doctor."

Now Gladys was getting pretty anxious. She continued with some further possible explanations for the disappearance of her husband. "He may have been kidnapped or he may have given someone a ride on the highway and they had done something to him." She also brought up Red Wells several more times in the conversation.

After saying all she dared to try to deflect suspicion away from Alvin, Gladys had Officer O'Brien give her a ride to the nearby ranch. En route they talked, and she described W.D. and Al to be "like brothers." She also said she had been a nurse in the service during WWII, and her husband had been a lieutenant in the war, and that he had a twin brother that was in the same outfit. She stated her husband was a very nice man but the twin brother was the cut-up. She said that when the twin brother wanted to leave camp that her husband would take his place and write his name — they write them the same way — and cover up for him. She stated her husband was killed in the service and this twin brother came back and was trying to take his place with her and become her husband.

They drove the cream-colored Chevrolet coupe Alvin had arrived in. Gladys also suggested they drive to Red Wells' place at old Shayville, because she suspected him; which they did, finding nothing. She said, "I feel we will find something there, due to the fact that Mr. Wells and the Doctor have had an awful argument and I feel he has been ambushed by Mr. Wells."

Gladys then asked Officer O'Brien if they had thought of a theory of kidnapping. He said no. She said, "It is a possibility, it could be. It is rumored that I brought 3 million dollars back from California, but it wasn't that much."

As they returned to the search site, Gladys asked O'Brien, "Are they holding him on suspicion?" He said, "Suspicion of what?" and she said, "I don't know." O'Brien asked her if Alvin had a car. She replied, "No, I don't think so." He said, "Well, I understood that he had an old car." She said, "Well, I have heard that he had one, but I have never seen it."

Officer O'Brien and Gladys drove up to the junction of the I-O-N Highway. Sheriff Glenn was there, and this was his first time to speak with her. O'Brien left and Sheriff Glenn and Gladys visited. The sheriff later testified, "She told me about her marriage to Doctor Broadhurst in the latter part of May 1946; said that they had gone together in Burley, Idaho, about 20 years ago; that they had been in love with each other ever since; and while they had married, both of them; in the meantime, they had stayed very much in love with one another; and she also told me that she had inherited money, approximately three million dollars; that it had been necessary for her to make a trip to California to take care of some estate business, and that Dr. Broadhurst had hired Williams to drive her down there. She said that after she and the doctor returned from California that his friends were congratulating him on the amount of money that she had inherited, that they had it Six Million Dollars but that was an error. It was just Three Million. She discussed the doctor's leaving his Caldwell home on Monday, said he left there about Monday noon in the pickup, pulling a trailer, and a saddle horse, going to their Jordan Valley ranch, where he was going to ride the cattle.

Gladys said she couldn't imagine what had happened to him. He was a big, strong, powerful man, and she suggested that it might be kidnapping, said he had the reputation of carrying large sums of money on his person at times; and she told him about Red Wells that the doctor had hired to work for him while he went hunting, and instead of him going to work he had gone to Oklahoma, claiming he had been called there on account of the death of his mother. She said the doctor was quite sore at Red over this, and also that Red owed the doctor some money, and the doctor wanted to collect that on the Monday before he left.

During that conversation Sheriff Glenn asked her where Mr. Williams was on Sunday and Monday, the 13th and 14th of October, and she said he was at their Caldwell ranch on Sunday. Sunday evening, she, the doctor, and Williams made a trip to Homedale to look at a trailer house. She and the doctor had planned on making a trip to Arizona later on. She said that most of Monday Williams was around the Caldwell ranch.

Gladys asked Sheriff Glenn if they had found anything. He said "Yes," and she enquired what it was. He told her it was some blood.

Sheriff Glenn then left Gladys and joined the other officers who were again talking to Clifford Dickson about the Model A Ford he had seen sitting by the side of the road all morning on Monday. Since he had spoken with the driver, Glenn then took Mr. Dickson to where Alvin was in the car with Sgt. Walker in the hope he could identify Alvin. Dickson and Alvin and Sgt. Walker sat in the car and chatted for a while. However, Dickson was not able to recognize Alvin definitely. Alvin was not wearing the same clothes, and that made Clifford uncertain.

After the officers finished with him, Gladys called Dickson over to sit in her car with her. She asked what he knew about the case. He said that Alvin was a suspect. Gladys told him it couldn't be Alvin, he hadn't done it, because he loved Dr. Broadhurst just like she did, and if he had done it, she would kill him like a dog. Lola was also in the car with them when Dickson said they suspected Alvin.

By now it was about three in the afternoon on Wednesday and no one had eaten since quite early, so the four police officers took Alvin and they went into Jordan Valley to Madriaga's for lunch. As they were finishing eating, Sheriff Glenn said he would go gas up the car.

As Charlie was paying for the gas at Pete Laca's service station, Gladys walked in.

"Are you through with Al now?" she asked.

"No, we are not."

"Are you holding him as a suspect?"

The sheriff replied, "We are holding him for questioning."

Gladys asked again, saying she had to have him to drive her car, and said she also needed him for the cattle, they were badly scattered.

"You'll have to make other arrangements on that. Mr. Williams cannot go with you," he replied.

George Vogt, a Caldwell neighbor, drove Gladys home from the search. "Mr. Vogt, I want to tell you that I know who killed Doc Broadhurst."

"Well," he said, "If you know who killed Doc Broadhurst, we had just better go right in and you tell it to the sheriff in town." He headed straight for the sheriff's office.

As they drove, Gladys told Vogt the twin brother story, and showed him the picture of the evil twin. So, he took her to Sheriff Moline of Canyon County where she blamed the evil twin brother, Lester. Gladys then told Sheriff Moline that Al had nothing to do with it, that he had no motive, and she thought the evil twin, Lester, was responsible. She said Lester's motive was a $2,000,000 estate in Nevada left to her by her father.

The sheriff listened patiently to everything Gladys had to say, taking careful notes and asking an occasional question to get the facts straight as she related them. He had his doubts, but A.A. was a professional and knew not to interrupt when someone is relating facts that may or may not have any truth to them.

"Sheriff, I appreciate so much you taking the time to listen to all these details," Gladys thanked him. "I have the greatest respect for you men who keep our communities safe. All my brothers but one are in law enforcement. One was an FBI agent in San Francisco and the others in Los Angeles."

Gladys is desperate to throw suspicion away from Alvin and onto anyone else. Moline was pretty skeptical about it all, but he didn't show a reaction to the things Gladys was saying.

Back in Oregon, Sheriff Glenn and Deputy Koopman took Alvin and drove the old Succor Creek road back to Vale, arriving at 6:45 PM. They stopped a number of times in steep places and looked for the body of Dr. Broadhurst, thinking it might have been thrown out and rolled down, but nothing was found. They are certain now they are looking for a body. Glenn drove, with Alvin in the front seat and Koopman in the back. They had dinner in Vale and then returned to the Sheriff's office about 7:30 PM for further questioning. They are making progress and see signs of Alvin breaking under the pressure. At 10:00 PM they called it a night, placing Alvin in jail and headed home for some much-needed sleep.

It has now been two days since the murder of Dr. W. D. Broadhurst, and the law is closing in fast.

CHAPTER 14

Wednesday evening there was a knock on the door of the Caldwell home, which was answered by Gladys. The hallway was dark and the visitor could not clearly see who had opened the door.

"Hello, Mrs. Adams, it is Grace Mowrey. I heard about Willis' disappearance and I just wanted to stop by to see if there is anything I can do. Is there any news?"

"No, this is Mrs. Broadhurst."

"Oh, I'm sorry, but I'm glad to meet you. The doctor and I are very dear friends. He has often had dinner with me in my home, and he is like a son to me. I've come to offer my sympathy and help. Is there any news of him?"

They went into the living room and Lola joined them from the kitchen. After a few minutes, Floyd came in from outside and welcomed their guest. "There is nothing you can do at this time that I can think of."

A thought came to Lola and she said, "Actually, there is something you can do. We want to go to a neighbor's for a few minutes and if you will sit here with Gladys for a bit, we will be very glad."

After Floyd and Lola were gone, Grace asked Gladys if she had ever lived in Caldwell before. Gladys replied with the story of how she and W.D. first met in Burley about 20 years earlier, then she smiled and said they were sweethearts for a time, but she had married someone else and the doctor left Burley and came to Caldwell to practice and they had not met again until shortly before they were married, perhaps in May, that she had business matters to settle up in Nevada and California and did not come back with the doctor at the time he came back, but he came back alone and she stayed a few weeks to settle up her business and then he came and brought her home with him.

Grace later testified, "The first real emotion she showed was in clasping her hands together and saying, 'What worries me the worst now, is that they have arrested my very best friend and have him in jail on suspicion.' That was a surprise to me for I hadn't heard of that, and I said, 'If he can prove where he was on that Monday, that will set him free.' She replied, 'I can do that, I could swear he worked right here around the barn all day Monday.'"

"'Then,' I said, 'that should be the least of your troubles.' She said 'Al wouldn't have killed the doctor, he just loved Doctor Broadhurst.' And, as I remember, that was all there was said about it at the time. She asked me to pardon her if she would go get the mail and look it over, that she had not seen it for a couple days. I said, 'Certainly.' So, she brought in a stack of letters, I suppose like that (indicating with her hands)."

When asked how high a stack of letters it was that Gladys brought in, Grace replied, "I don't know how many, two or three dozen it looked to me like. I didn't pay a great deal of attention to those letters for I did not suspicion her at all, but she looked through the letters rather nervously, piled them up here and there. While she was looking over the mail, Doctor and Mrs. Adams came in and our conversation together ceased."

CHAPTER 15

Lola later testified that on the next morning, Thursday, October 17, 1946, Gladys "came running through the house and ran into the bedroom to me; she was crying, the tears were streaming down her face; she had a note in her hand. It seemed that she had gone to let the dog out the front door and had seen the note tucked under the front door. She brought it to me to read, and said, 'This is from my dead husband's twin brother.'"

The note read:

> "Your cowboy strongarm didn't do it, but don't start anything or I'll get you same as I did Doctor. I warned you and I need some cash. Sweet Pea."

Lola continued her testimony, "Gladys also told me the twin brother had threatened her life many times, and just recently, just before the doctor had gone hunting, she had seen him in the yard, and he had threatened her life, and the doctor's too. She said he had beaten her on several occasions in California, and he had wanted to marry her to get a portion of this estate that was supposed to have been left to her."

After relating all this to Lola, Gladys and Lola drove into town with the note and went to Sheriff Moline of Caldwell. Gladys brought along a photograph that had written on the back "Les's twin brother, Lester Melvin Lincoln."

"I know this note is from Lester," said Gladys. "It's in his writing, and I know because I've seen his writing many times. I think he is in town, and I'm frightened. He came by the house about a day before the doctor left for his hunting trip, and he threatened me then."

"What is the meaning of 'Sweet Pea?'" asked the sheriff.

"That's a nickname Leslie used to call Lester. He's a real psychopath and he's been in the mental hospital as a psychopathic case."

"Well, most likely fingerprints will be found on this note. In order to eliminate your fingerprints, we'd like to get your prints on file, both of you. Would you object to being fingerprinted?"

Neither of the ladies had any objection, so the sheriff directed them to go with Deputy Hale down to the basement where their fingerprints would be taken. As they prepared to leave his office, Sheriff Moline asked Gladys about the case in California, if a summons had been served upon her. She said no, she had torn up the summons and the case had been thrown out of court.

The state later proved that this "Sweet Pea" note was in Gladys' handwriting on stationary she owned. Her desperation is growing as she sees the law officers coming closer to the truth by the hour. The photograph was later determined to be a picture of Leslie, her real fifth husband.

Meanwhile, in Oregon, the law officers were making progress. Sgt. Walker and Officer O'Brien requested permission to meet with Alvin in the jail in Vale, to where they were admitted. After lengthy and intense interrogation, Alvin finally broke down and confessed to the murder of Doctor W. D. Broadhurst. He gave them full details of the events of Monday, October 14th, including the killing and disposal of the body and other evidence.

With Sheriff Glenn's permission, Walker and O'Brien took Alvin and drove to the scene of the crime. They went about 11 miles south of Homedale Junction. They drove roughly 300 yards off the highway to the SW, then got out and continued another 100 yards on foot. Alvin showed them where W.D.'s body was lying in a wash, covered with sagebrush. They were careful not to disturb the body or the scene at that time.

Alvin then took them to where the murder weapon had been hidden, which was an old Stevens single-shot shotgun. It had been broken down and stuffed down a badger hole out in the sagebrush. Alvin got on his hands and knees and started digging in the dirt there. He pulled out some sagebrush, then the butt of a gun, then the barrel.

The trio returned to Vale where Alvin was again placed in the jail cell at 3:15 PM on October 17th. An hour and a half later, Alvin was taken from his cell to a room in the courthouse where Sheriff Glenn, Sgt. Walker and District Attorney E. Otis Smith questioned him at length for information not only about the killing itself, but also about all events that led up to this heinous act. It turned out to be a long, tiring session lasting four and a half hours. This meeting was recorded by the court reporter, William Walker.

At the same time, the other law officers were busy at work on other aspects of the case. Deputy Koopman and Officer O'Brien picked up a photographer in Ontario named Johnny Estano, after which they met Sheriff Moline and Deputy Hale from Idaho at the crime scene. Dr. Floyd Adams was asked to be there also. The group returned to the location where W.D.'s body had been stashed. Johnny was directed to take multiple photographs of the body, before it was moved. Floyd was tasked with confirming this was the body of Willis, which he did. After finishing these necessary requirements, W.D.'s body was loaded into an ambulance and taken to the Peckham Funeral Home in Caldwell. Floyd was admonished to tell no one of the events of that evening, as doing so might jeopardize their case.

Gladys is equally busy. As she senses that Alvin is in danger, which by extension means she is in danger, she is taking more desperate measures. She visits a young man named Rufus Lanphear, a friend of Alvin's, and persuades him to claim that Alvin was with Rufus on Monday at 2:00 PM, buying an auto part from him. Gladys then has her attorney, Cleve Groome, take her and Rufus to Vale to give this new evidence to Sheriff Glenn. Mrs. Latham, mother to Rufus, insisted on accompanying them also.

The arrival of Gladys and her entourage created a logistical problem for Sheriff Glenn and those still interrogating Alvin. The sheriff's office and the jail were located in the courthouse building, which was constructed in 1902 and was woefully in need of expansion and remodeling.

Not wanting either Gladys or Alvin to even see that they were meeting with the other party, the Sheriff had to think fast.

"Mr. Groome, will you and Mrs. Broadhurst and the others please wait on these benches here in the hall while I go upstairs to find a good place for us to meet to discuss your business?" asked Charlie. "It will only take a minute or two."

He hustled back upstairs to the courtroom where they were meeting with Alvin. Sgt. Walker and Alvin moved into the library and closed the door. William Walker, the court reporter and the District Attorney remained in the courtroom while Sheriff Glenn escorted Gladys and her party into the courtroom. Once they were seated and the doors closed, Sgt. Walker took Alvin and returned him to his jail cell. Neither party seemed to be aware of the presence of the other.

"Now, what can we do for you folks this evening?" asked the sheriff.

Cleve Groome made the first statement. "Sheriff, there is some information we think you should have, and that is why we are here this evening. First, Mrs. Broadhurst would like to tell you of a threatening note she received this morning which could shed some light on who might have killed Dr. Broadhurst. She took this note to Sheriff Moline in Caldwell this morning, along with a picture of the author of that note. I'll let her fill you in on the details."

Gladys then repeated the story of the "Sweet Pea" note and told Sheriff Glenn all about her deceased husband's twin brother and his mistreatment of her, how he beat her and twice had hurt her so badly she had to go to the hospital. She then said that both the letter and the photo had been turned over to Sheriff Moline in Caldwell.

Groome then discussed the whereabouts of Alvin Williams on the day Doctor Broadhurst disappeared. Rufus claimed that Alvin had come to his place shortly after noon on Monday and that he had come there for a part for his car. But the part Rufus had was for a '28 Model A and Williams wanted a part for a '29 Model A, so he wouldn't take it. He had handled it, however, and he wanted the Sheriff to take the car part and check it for fingerprints to prove that Alvin was at his place shortly after noon on Monday, staying until about 2:30 PM.

DA Otis Smith responded, "Well, I guess that pretty well establishes where Williams was at that time."

Gladys then went on to tell the sheriff and the DA that Alvin had been at the Caldwell ranch Monday morning until noon. "So, he couldn't have been there unless he had an airoplane."

Gladys and her group left the courthouse that evening feeling they had accomplished something. They had accomplished one thing: Sheriff Charlie Glenn knew they were all a pack of liars, and he was more convinced than ever that Gladys was the real culprit, and probably the mastermind behind this killing. It occurred to him that Mrs. Broadhurst had come to him trying to prove that Alvin had not been at the scene of the crime at the time of the killing, when in fact it had not been revealed to her or anyone else that it had been proven that there even was a killing. Or what was the actual time and location of the killing. Or that Alvin had made a statement. She obviously knew more than she was supposed to know. That information had to have been given to her by the killer.

Later in the trial, Rufus Lanphear completely repudiated his alibi for Alvin. He admitted he had made a false statement to the sheriff and District Attorney.

After Gladys and her supporters left, the officers completed getting Alvin's statement written down and signed by Alvin Lee Williams. Alvin went back to jail; Gladys went to bed.

CHAPTER 16

By Friday morning, the good doctor's sisters, Annie Adams and Sarah Allen, had arrived from St. Anthony, Idaho, to be with the family during this ordeal. Sarah suggested that Gladys ought to give Sheriff Moline a call to see if there had been any further developments in the case. Up to this point, it had not been revealed that Alvin had confessed, nor even that they had found the body.

"Sheriff, this is Mrs. Broadhurst on the phone. We are all waiting here for any news, and we are sick at heart that nobody knows anything. Can you tell us any news at all? Has anything been found of my husband? Are there any answers?"

"Yes, ma'am, I'm very sorry to have to tell you that we have found your husband's body. He has been murdered."

After relating this terrible news to the family, Gladys began to wail. Crying, she kept repeating, "Oh, oh, I loved him so much!"

Gladys spent the rest of the day Friday in bed, but about 5:30 PM Sheriff Moline arrived and asked Gladys if she had any objection to accompanying him to Vale to meet with Sheriff Glenn and his officers. She agreed, dressed for the trip, and they drove to Vale.

The purpose of the meeting in Vale was for the law officers to interrogate Gladys and try to break her down to confessing to her complicity in the murder of her husband. Yet, she was surprisingly strong, and would not agree with their accusations about her. Gladys insisted it had to be her dead husband's evil twin brother, or perhaps Red Wells, or perhaps some stranger who had murdered her husband. She completely deflected all attempts to trap her in any inconsistency or admit to any involvement in the death of Doctor Broadhurst. The officers knew it, but they could not get her to admit it.

Sheriff Moline finally drove Gladys back to Caldwell around 11:30 PM, but instead of taking her home they went to the Canyon County courthouse where he continued to grill her for another four hours. Although he made no progress on getting Gladys to confess, he arrested her and placed Gladys in jail at 3:30 AM the morning of October 19th, 1946.

The question for which there doesn't seem to be an answer is why Sheriff Glenn didn't arrest Gladys when she was in Oregon at the Vale courthouse? Why did he allow Sheriff Moline to take her back to Idaho? What changed between 11:30 PM and 3:30 AM that enabled Sheriff Moline in Caldwell, Idaho to make the decision to arrest Gladys? If she had been arrested in Vale, extradition would not have been necessary, which would have saved a lot of time, money, and aggravation.

Gladys was in jail, but she would not make it easy on those trying to hold her responsible for the death of her husband. Gladys refused to waive extradition, which meant she sat in the Canyon County, Idaho jail for two months while her attorneys fought the state at every step of the process. While fighting the extradition, Gladys engaged the services of veteran Ontario, Oregon attorney Patrick "P.J." Gallagher as her lead attorney. Gallagher would ultimately collaborate with her previous attorneys, Cleve Groome of Caldwell and Darold D. (D.D.) DeCoe of Sacramento. He also asked attorney William H. Langroise of Boise to join the defense team.

Dr. Willis David Broadhurst was given two funerals for those who loved him to be able to show their love for the family and their grief at losing such a good and kind friend. The first funeral was held in Caldwell on Monday, October

21st and was attended by several hundred persons, including W.D.'s hunting companion, District Judge Thomas E. Buckner, who adjourned court that day to be able to attend. Gladys' brother Jess acted as an honorary pallbearer and the eulogy was given by Dr. H. H. Hayman of the College of Idaho. After the funeral, Gladys was visited in jail by two of her brothers who had come to attend the funeral: Captain Jess Ralphs of the Reno, NV fire department and Tony Ralphs of Truckee, CA.

The second funeral was held the next day in Parker, Idaho and Bishop Oakley Hunter of the Heman Ward of the LDS church officiated at the services at the Parker LDS chapel. W.D. was buried in the Parker Memorial Park in Parker, Idaho.

At the same time as W.D.'s second funeral, Gladys informed Sheriff Moline that she was tired of wearing the same clothes every day. She needed to go back to the house to get some clean changes of clothing to wear. In what seems to be a mind-boggling decision, the sheriff agreed to take her back to the house so she could get some personal items for her use in the jail. Thus, accompanied by attorney Groome and Deputy Hale, the four went to the Caldwell home.

Lola and the children were home when they arrived at the house. Gladys asked to go to her bedroom to collect the things she wanted to take with her back to the jail. Amazingly, Sheriff Moline allowed her to go into her bedroom and close the door while in there. It took some time for Gladys to emerge, and the lawmen and her attorney sat in the living room and visited with Lola until Gladys reappeared.

Lola later testified, "She took a lot of papers and letters and books, in a little box I had given her. She also took my pillow." The box was a 10" x 10" x 3" deep pasteboard box decorated all over with poinsettia flowers. Gladys also took a small suitcase filled with clothing and toiletry items.

Sheriff Moline took note of the poinsettia box and told Gladys, "You can't just take that into the jail with you, you know. If you want to take it with you, it is subject to search before it goes in." Gladys pivoted toward her attorney and handed the box to him. "Here, Cleve, please take this for me," she said, and he tucked the box under his arm.

Back to jail she went, but now with many more choices of wardrobe to wear each day. Appearances are important to Gladys. Because she is fighting extradition, Gladys ends up spending two full months in jail in Caldwell.

The Klamath Falls *Herald and News* reported that Gladys is "taking it easy" reading current events magazines in jail in Caldwell. But things aren't really going all that smoothly in Caldwell. Where there is Gladys, there is drama. Lots of drama.

Now that both of the conspirators are in jail, it is lawyer time as both sides begin their work. W.D.'s will was filed for probate by Cleve Groome. This is the will that the good doctor created at his wife's insistence less than three weeks before his death, leaving his entire estate "to my beloved wife, Gladys Elaine Broadhurst." Four days later, W.D.'s three sisters announce they plan to contest the will.

There are now two matters that could stand between Gladys and W.D.'s significant wealth: the contesting of the will by the sisters and the announced decision by the District Attorney that they plan to seek the death penalty in the trial of Mrs. Gladys Broadhurst.

District Attorney E. Otis Smith, who participated in the interrogation of Alvin and his subsequent confession, is at the end of his term. A new District Attorney, Charles W. Swan, has been elected and will take office in the new year, and the young DA will be in charge of one of the highest profile cases in America at the time. The two DA's realize Mr. Swan needs some help, and they select an experienced trial lawyer to assist them in the preparation and prosecution of this important trial. Blaine Hallock of the Baker, Oregon law firm Blaine, Hallock & Banta is engaged as a special prosecutor for the state.

Lola is likewise staying busy. Her dislike for Gladys has escalated into intense hatred, for good reason, and she is determined to do whatever she can to aid the prosecution in their quest for justice. She is particularly chagrined that Gladys made off with whatever was in the poinsettia box. Hoping to find some evidence that would be useful to the prosecution, Lola searched the whole house carefully to see if there was anything to be found that would help the state's case. She checked in Gladys' bedroom, the basement, and anywhere else that seemed likely. Lola was particularly interested in finding letters and telegrams between Willis and Gladys such as she had seen Gladys sorting prior to her arrest.

During the trial, Lola was asked, "After the defendant had been incarcerated at Caldwell, did you make any further effort to locate papers and documents in the home?"

"Yes, sir; I did."

"And what did you ultimately discover?"

"Well, I couldn't find a lot of the papers I had previously seen in the doctor's bedroom, on his dresser."

"And did you make any search in this bedroom, Number 2?"

"Yes, sir, I did," Lola answered.

"And what did you note there, if anything?"

"Well, I was in the room, looking around, and I noticed fingerprints on the top of the hot air ventilator, near the floor. I was just wondering and curious about those fingerprints, after I had noticed them, and I just pushed the cover back and noticed a lot of bits of torn scraps in the bottom of the ventilator."

"What did you do about that?"

"I recognized one piece of an envelope, I recognized it as one I had seen on the doctor's dresser sometime back."

"What did you do with the fragment?" asked the DA.

"I called Sheriff Moline at Caldwell and asked if he could come out to the house."

When Lola advised the sheriff of what she found, he contacted Sheriff Glenn in Vale, who drove to Caldwell to join Sheriff Moline. Sgt. Walker and Charles Swan, the District Attorney-elect also came along and they all drove to the Broadhurst place. Lola let them in, led them into Gladys' bedroom and pointed out the register. Sgt. Walker got down on his hands and knees and removed the vent cover. He could see some scraps of paper, and reaching in he found quite a pile of bits of paper hidden in the air duct about two feet from the opening. The paper scraps made a nice little pile when he got them all out.

The law officers encouraged Lola to contact them again if she found any other items that might be used in their prosecution of the case. Sheriff Glenn took the sack of scraps back to Vale, where he and Sgt. Walker and Charles Swan worked at reconstructing the puzzles of torn paper, taping them together with Scotch tape.

Ultimately, the material found in the register duct proved to be four letters and some blank stationary that matched the paper on which the "Sweet Pea" note was written. During the trial, the state used these exhibits to help demonstrate that Gladys was the author of the "Sweet Pea" note.

The four taped-up letters all turned out to be letters Gladys had written W.D. from California while she and Alvin were traveling around. One of them was dated August 8, 1946:

```
Truckee, CA 8/8/46

Big Chief Camp, Box 625, Truckee,
Cal

Darling, Darling, Darling,

     I miss you, I love you. How much
is as the vastness of the blue blue
sky here. Forgive me honey please for
not wanting you to come at this time,
```

it's so beautiful here, it hurts one's eyes. Al is overwhelmed. He's speechless. He wants to stay here. He is opening shingles for Tony. He drove very well, but it was so hot we nearly died. Will come back in the night. We got a parking ticket at Reno on Monday. Never did find out why??

I go to court Monday 10 AM – going before another judge – would have gone yesterday, but Tony is ill. Has been working too hard. We played together the other night & really had a time so spect he is tired. He was so happy to see me he cried. He looks fine tho, but stomach is haywire. Needs a course with my daddy. They were amazed how good I looked. Had my hair fixed nice at Reno, & so mommie just looked her best for her brother.

How I appreciate you darling. I know how hard it was to let me go, but soon we can go together always.

Don't work too hard darling. I miss you at nite always snuggling up to my honey – it's cold here and no daddy.

Will write again tomorrow Darling. Helping Gwynie today. Help is short. Write me here precious. I love you, I adore you, my darling my dearest man in the world.

Love from us all
Your lil mommie wife

Gladys obviously judged that these letters would be viewed negatively if they came to light, so she attempted to dispose of them in the heat register. That attempt was probably more harmful to her than if she had just left them sitting in the dresser drawer.

Negative news is proliferating for Gladys, however. On October 26th, Superior Court Judge Peter J. Shields granted an interlocutory decree of divorce to Leslie M. Lincoln from his wife, Gladys. In California in 1946, interlocutory divorces were granted, which became final one year after that date. According to a news article in the *Ogden Standard Examiner* the following day,

"Lincoln charged in an amended complaint filed last June that that Mrs. Broadhurst, whom he had married on Jan. 2, 1942, married Broadhurst in Reno on May 20. 'She returned the next day,' he said, 'and they continued to live as man and wife until June 2, when he discovered she had married the rancher in Reno.'" Lincoln's attorney also stated that Doctor Broadhurst was Gladys' sixth husband.

Now the public knew not only that Gladys was a bigamist, but that she had married six times. Sheriff Glenn and the District Attorney also know that Gladys married a seventh time when she married Alvin, but this information has not yet been divulged to the news media.

By this time, Gladys was finding other outlets in her desperate attempts to elicit sympathy for her cause. The extradition request from the State of Oregon was still pending and under consideration by Governor Arnold Williams of Idaho. What she needed was some public sentiment on her side. The next announcement from her attorney was a bombshell.

October 31, 1946
PRESS RELEASE

On behalf of Mrs. Gladys Ralphs Broadhurst I wish to state that I am advised by her physician that a child will be born to Gladys Ralphs

Broadhurst and her late husband, Dr.
W. D. Broadhurst.

Cleve Groome, attorney.
Caldwell, Idaho

The month of November passed by rather quietly, with Gladys sitting in jail in Caldwell and Alvin doing the same in Vale. The law officers in Oregon were working hard to put all the pieces together on Gladys' very convoluted life and her relationship with Alvin. P.J. Gallagher and his defense team were working equally hard to get their case ready to defend Gladys. The first order of business was the extradition. If they could persuade the Idaho governor that her arrest was unwarranted and unsubstantiated by the facts, they may be able to prevent Gladys from ever being on trial in Oregon. That was their fondest hope, but it was a long shot.

December turned out to have all the newsworthy excitement that November lacked. On December 5th, Sheriff Charles Glenn delivered to Governor Arnold Williams of Idaho a warrant for extradition for Gladys. The warrant claims Gladys is an "accessory after the fact of first-degree murder." It charges that Gladys aided Alvin Lee Williams, Parma, in attempting to escape trial, conviction and punishment in the death of Dr. Broadhurst. The governor held a brief hearing on the matter at the time the warrant was delivered to get an understanding of the position of each side.

The newspaper reported "Attorneys P.J. Gallagher, Ontario and Cleve Groome, Caldwell representing the attractive titian-haired widow, contended that the Idaho executive should deny extradition on the grounds that the extradition warrant had not sufficiently charged her with the crime." Governor Arnold took the matter under advisement and will rule on it in due course. He set a date for a full hearing on the matter for December 9th, but at the request of Cleve Groome, it was later postponed until the 11th.

On the same day the warrant was presented to the governor, perhaps as a reaction to the possibility of extradition, Gladys was taken from jail and placed in a local hospital "for observation." The stated cause for the need for observation was that Gladys received a fright after seeing a rat in her jail cell. The newspaper reported that "she is expecting a child, is not seriously ill but was taken from the Canyon County jail to the hospital to safeguard her health." It is claimed that Gladys is now five months pregnant, or "five months gone," as one newspaper termed it. She ends up spending two weeks in the hospital, and her attorney Groome reported that "the event could have affected her pregnancy."

There is no further mention of Gladys being pregnant, and she never gave birth to a child.

The next big excitement in December occurred on the 18th. After a week of consideration, the governor is prepared to issue a ruling on the warrant for extradition. In a "cat and mouse" game, the attorneys for the defense were prepared with plans for immediate response to a decision to grant the warrant.

Plan one will be to submit a petition for habeas corpus to the Canyon County judge as soon as he formalizes the warrant for extradition. Habeas corpus is a process of law in which a person can report an unlawful detention or imprisonment to a court, requesting the court to order the custodian of the person (usually a prison official) to bring the prisoner into the court so that the judge can hold a hearing and determine whether the detention is lawful. P.J. hopes the courts will agree that there is insufficient evidence to hold Gladys for trial.

However, anticipating the unlikely event that the habeas corpus will be approved, P.J. and his colleagues prepared a motion for appeal of that decision, and brought with them a check for $300 for bond, a required element.

Things progressed as anticipated, but the state was one jump ahead of the defense attorneys. The governor of Idaho, Arnold Williams, granted extradition. PJ Gallagher and Cleve Groome filed their petition for habeas corpus, which the Caldwell judge Thomas Buckner denied. Having anticipated that, the attorneys were ready with their appeal and produced their bond check for $300.

However, it so happened that Judge Buckner had been a close personal friend of Doctor Broadhurst, was a regular participant on their annual hunting trips, and had even adjourned court the afternoon of W.D.'s funeral so he could serve as an honorary pall bearer at the funeral, where he also gave a eulogy. Apparently, in the 1940's, judges did not recuse themselves due to a conflict of interest!

Thus, not only did Judge Buckner deny the petition for habeas corpus, he also advised the attorneys their check would not be accepted as bond, and while they were arguing that point, the transfer of Gladys from Canyon County officials to Malheur County officials was consummated.

Granddad was outsmarted that time! It is difficult to avoid the conclusion that the judge and the two sheriffs worked closely together to ensure the extradition took place at that time.

Gladys was ushered into what would be her new resting place for the next three months: the Malheur County Jail in Vale, Oregon.

CHAPTER 17

A trial date of February 24, 1947 was scheduled for Gladys Broadhurst by Judge M. A. Biggs, to be held in the County Courthouse in Vale. A trial date for Alvin Lee Williams for first degree murder was also postponed from February 3rd to March 10th, to enable Alvin to give his testimony against Gladys before he goes on trial.

Both sides in the case have a tremendous workload ahead of them in preparation for this trial, which will be one of the most sensational cases ever held in Eastern Oregon. The prosecution does a marvelous job of learning everything there is to know about Gladys, her marital history, her marriage to the doctor, and her relationship with Alvin. By the time of the trial, they think they know more about Gladys than she knows herself.

District Attorney Swan and Sheriff Glenn traveled to Sacramento to join up with Joe Lannon, the Chief Criminal Investigator for Sacramento County to interrogate Leslie Lincoln. They met in Lincoln's attorney's office for that meeting. Leslie confirmed he had no twin brother, nor any brothers at all. He also consented to having his fingerprints taken and consented that the authorities may obtain his fingerprints from the War Dept. of the U.S. for comparison purposes.

In an interview with the press, Judge Biggs says that if the jury finds Gladys guilty of murder in the first degree and makes no recommendation, she would automatically be sentenced to death in the Oregon gas chamber. DA Charles Swan said he would ask that the jury sentence her to death.

However, the State of Oregon had never executed a woman up to that time.

The attorneys for the defense have an even greater challenge on their hands. One big challenge is to find a jury of 12 men and women who can look at this case impartially. With all the lurid publicity surrounding this case, can they find any jurors who have not already reached a preconceived opinion about the guilt of Gladys Broadhurst? And can they likewise find jurors who don't view divorce as an unpardonable sin — especially six divorces? And how can they determine that a juror wouldn't view bigamy as a clear indication of the moral turpitude of a woman?

As would be expected, Gladys is having a difficult time sitting in jail waiting for the trial to begin. She adamantly continues to proclaim her innocence, claiming she had nothing to do with the murder of her beloved husband. In a telephone interview with the *Idaho Daily Statesman*, Gladys says she has not been permitted to see Alvin. She also said, "I just wish I could get it over with one way or the other".

However, Gladys also related, "The people all over the country have been wonderful... I've received many flowers and countless letters. Then, too, many members of the Mormon Church, of which I am a member, have been over to see me."

The trial began on February 24th as scheduled with selection of a jury. On the fourth day, a jury of nine men and three women was empaneled. Judge Biggs sent them home for the evening with instructions to gather up enough clothing to last for the duration of the trial, which ended up lasting three full weeks. Up to this time they have been allowed to go home each evening, but for the duration of the trial they stayed in the hotel at night, under the watchful eyes of sheriff's deputies.

The defense attorneys moved to have any discussion of Gladys' previous marriages excluded. Motion denied.

They moved to have any mention of bigamy excluded. The defense objected that she was not on trial for bigamy and this would prejudice the jury, but the prosecution countered that it all linked together in the intricate murder plot. Motion denied.

The attorneys for the defense moved for a summary acquittal and argued that Gladys was arrested without a warrant and that officers took papers from her room without a search warrant. PJ said she was arrested "unjustifiably since she had committed 'no crime' in his (W.D.'s) presence." Motion denied.

Gallagher also moved that all papers taken by the officers from Gladys' bedroom be excluded from evidence and returned to the defendant, again since she was arrested without a warrant for her arrest and the documents were taken without a search warrant. Motion denied.

The prosecuting attorney did wish, however, that they had possession of whatever papers had been in the poinsettia box, but the officers had never been able to locate them.

PJ Gallagher objected to any testimony being given by Alvin. Gallagher's argument was:

"The basis of this objection (to Alvin being permitted to testify) is sort of two-fold. The first point that I desire to present is that this proffered witness is a co-defendant with the defendant on trial, indicted for the same crime, both of them subject to the same punishment, both principals in the commission of the same crime under the laws of the State of Oregon.

That is one point, and the second point is that if treated otherwise than that he would have to be treated as an accomplice -- if that would qualify him, which I contend it would not -- and he would be incompetent to testify at this time as an accomplice because there has been no concert of action proven by any evidence at the present time."

Judge Biggs ruled on this question: "I am going to hold that it is going to be the duty of the State to show at least a prima facie case of conspiracy before Williams will be permitted to testify." In the end, however, the prosecution was able to satisfy the judge on this score and Alvin became the star witness for the prosecution.

Alvin told everything. He testified that Gladys had made the first advances toward him, that she was the one who first broached the idea of murdering her husband, that she was in all respects the motivation and the motivator for this crime. He gave full details of all of his actions on the October day that culminated in the death of Doctor Broadhurst.

Alvin answered "yes" in a voice that nearly broke when District Attorney Charles Swan asked, "did you love Mrs. Broadhurst?"

On cross-examination, PJ asked Alvin if he wasn't "pretty satisfied" with himself as ranch hand and lover, Williams replied, "Well, I wasn't complaining any."

The prosecution rested, and the defense rested without calling any witnesses of their own.

In the prosecution's closing arguments, District Attorney Charles Swan argued, "She is the one who conceived, planned and directed the perpetration of this monstrous crime. The hand that raised the wrench and pulled the trigger on the shotgun was the hand of the defendant. It was the fulfillment of what she planned."

Swan said that Williams was virtually "her slave" and he acted as "her agent" in the murder's commission. He said, "It is reasonable now to infer that Williams was under the control and domination of the defendant . . . He loved her . . . . He saw a new life . . . he was her slave."

Special Prosecutor Hallock referred to Alvin as "a man with the mind of a 12-year-old boy." He painted Alvin as easy pickings for a woman such as the defendant. He drew a snicker from the audience and a wide grin from Gallagher when he said, "You have seen her here in the court room exerting her powerful personality on the stalwart group of men serving as her defense counsel!"

In the defense's closing arguments, PJ Gallagher pictured Gladys as "a woman whose moral sense was dimmed by continual sin and use of drugs, but she was completely innocent of murder." PJ shouted, "There was no deal to kill Dr. Broadhurst. Williams thought of murder on his own account when he realized he could no longer sleep with the boss' wife."

PJ said Alvin's attorneys had attempted through his testimony to "walk around the gas chamber instead of into it."

Gallagher also quoted from the Gospel of John the story of the adulteress who was brought to Jesus. "Take the adulteries out of this case and you haven't got enough left to wad the shotgun that Williams killed the doctor with!" Gallagher shouted.

Thelma Clegg, who was covering the trial for the *Ontario Argus*, wrote: "Thursday the last act began, with P. J. Gallagher and Blaine Hallock having a final say. Gallagher played his role to the fullest. He spoke eloquently, pounding his fists, and paced the floor. I think he enjoyed the part as much as did the spectators. At one time, when he referred to Mrs. B as the 'little girl' his face drew down and he seemed on the verge of tears. He attacked, with gusto, the character of the two star witnesses, Williams and Mrs. Adams; and scathingly compared the D.A. to a bloodhound out after a rabbit. He denounced the way the stories of the 'titian beauty sleeping with the hired man' had been played up, and how the scandal-hungry mob outside the courtroom hissed at the 'little girl' as she was taken through them. He bemoaned his inability and poor talents and said he would always feel he could have done more if she was sentenced. As he walked back and sat down, Gladys reached out and clasped his hand with much show of feeling."

One editor wrote, "Newspaper reporters praised the oratorical effort of Pat Gallagher in the woman's defense, but while it may have been good oratory it did not prove convincing logic to the jury." (*The Oregon Statesman*, 3/13/47, editorial by Charles A. Sprague)

If the jurors didn't enter the trial with any preconceived ideas of guilt or innocence, by the time the trial concluded, their minds were made up. The jury was out for only 3 hours and 23 minutes. It took 3 ballots for the jurors to reach a conclusion, but all jurors favored "guilty" from the beginning. The only discussion focused on the penalty. On the first ballot: 5 for death, 7 for life. On the second ballot: 1 for death, 11 for life. On the third ballot: unanimous for life.

No. 455. VERDICT—CRIMINAL—GUILTY   Printed and for Sale by Glass & Prudhomme Co., Portland, Ore.

In the Circuit Court of the State of Oregon,

For the County of ___Malheur___

THE STATE OF OREGON
Against   #677

                                                       ACCUSED OF THE CRIME OF

___Gladys Broadhurst___   First Degree Murder
           Defendant .

We, the Jury impaneled and sworn to try the guilt or innocence of the above named defendant , find the said defendant ___Gladys Broadhurst___

guilty of the crime ___of Murder in the First Degree___
                                                       as charged in the indictment
___and do recommend life imprisonment___   ___Ed Oakes___ Foreman.

The verdict was expected by most observers, but many were extremely unhappy about the decision not to impose the death penalty. "Some of our brethren of the press are complaining about Mrs. Broadhurst escaping the death sentence and are blaming it onto the jury which convicted her. Perhaps the jury was influenced by the same thing that got for Mrs. Broadhurst her seven husbands." – *Corvallis Gazette-Times*, March 17, 1947.

Gladys Broadhurst was transported by Sheriff Charles W. Glenn to the Oregon State Penitentiary in Salem, Oregon on March 27, 1947. Mrs. Glenn accompanied them and served as Matron for the trip. Gladys was a model prisoner and excelled at teaching other inmates many skills such as cooking, sewing, and playing the accordion and piano.

Leslie M. Lincoln's divorce from Gladys became final on October 30, 1947 while Gladys was in prison in Salem. The interlocutory decree had been granted one year prior.

Two days after Gladys was convicted, Alvin Lee Williams was allowed to plead "Guilty" to murder in the second degree and was sentenced to life in prison. At his sentencing, Judge Biggs said Alvin's testimony at Gladys' trial was "very material," and went on to say, "I am convinced that had there been no Gladys Broadhurst there would have been no crime. He (Williams) was a tool in the hands of the defendant. I do not feel that this defendant under any circumstances should receive greater punishment than Gladys Broadhurst." Alvin also served his time in the Oregon State Penitentiary.

The attorneys for the defense appealed Gladys' conviction to the Oregon Supreme Court. The arguments were heard on May 18, 1948, but the trial decision was affirmed by that court.

A petition was filed in U.S. Supreme Court in February of 1949 for writ of certiorari: Gladys Broadhurst vs. State of Oregon. But on May 16 of that year the U.S. Supreme Court denied Mrs. Gladys Broadhurst a review of her Malheur County, Oregon first degree murder conviction.

There were still legal matters requiring resolution, however. Doctor Broadhurst's three sisters had contested the will leaving 100% of W.D.'s estate to Gladys. After much negotiation, the parties agreed to settle the matter without going to court. The sisters received two-thirds of the estate and Gladys received one-third, which amounted to $51,000.

That was a significant sum in 1947. At that time, the Federal Minimum Wage was 40 cents per hour. The average annual income was $2,600.

The Gallagher family saying was, "She got life and we got the ranch." That wasn't literally true, but there may have been a kernel of truth in it. Undoubtedly the bulk of Gladys' inheritance went toward her legal bills, which were substantial considering not only the trial but the two appeals. It is true that shortly after the conclusion of this trial PJ Gallagher and Martin Gallagher constructed and opened their law firm's new office building on SW First Street in Ontario. Some of the locals referred to it tongue-in-cheek as "The Broadhurst Building."

CHAPTER 18

How long is "life?" How long should a convicted murderer serve in prison when sentenced to "life?" In the case of Gladys Broadhurst, "life" amounted to 9 years and 4 months. She was paroled on July 27, 1956.

Alvin Lee Williams entered the State Penitentiary on May 14, 1947 and was paroled on August 14th, 1957. His "life" sentence amounted to 10 years and 3 months.

At the time of her parole, Gladys Broadhurst had just turned 50 years old the month prior. What was she now going to do with the rest of her life?

```
SALEM, OR 15 JANUARY 1961 1330 HRS
TO: LEO JOHN O'SHEA, SACRAMENTO, CA
VIA: WESTERN UNION

DEAREST LEO: MEMORIES OF OUR NIGHTS
TOGETHER SO MANY YEARS AGO STILL
FLOOD MY DREAMS TODAY. STOP. I HAVE
NEVER FORGOTTEN YOU. STOP. HOW COULD
I EVER FORGET A MAN LIKE YOU? STOP.
I'D LOVE TO TELL YOU MY STORY. STOP.
PLEASE WRITE WITH YOUR ADDRESS IF
INTERESTED:
      GLADYS RALPHS BROADHURST
      111 OREGON ST.
      SALEM, OR

STOP.
```
The End

EPILOGUES

EPILOGUE 1 – FINAL MARRIAGES

Gladys Lincoln married her eighth husband, Leo John O'Shea, in Marion County, Oregon on May 2, 1961. Marion County is where Oregon's state capitol and state prison are located. The date is almost five years after Gladys was paroled.

Gladys and Leo returned to Sacramento where they lived together until her death on August 14, 1973.

After his parole on August 14, 1957, Alvin Williams and Nina Cantrell were married in Canyon County, Idaho on July 1, 1959. They raised a family and lived together until Alvin's death on May 26, 2010.

EPILOGUE 2 – HEADSTONES

Today's world has changed light years from 1946 when the good Doctor W.D. Broadhurst met his demise. One dramatic change is that gaining information was a major task in 1946 that required a lot of digging and a lot of patience. Today, a world of information is at our finger tips.

For example, and this is an amazing thing, we can go online at billiongraves.com and find details about the burial place of just about anybody in the United States. In fact, many of those details include a photo of the headstone placed over the deceased's final resting place. This is true of Leo and Gladys O'Shea.

Amazingly, even after her death, Gladys was the center of controversy. There is a strange anomaly about the headstone for Leo and Gladys. As is customary over the graves of married couples, both the husband and the wife are listed on one shared headstone. Thus, when I searched for Gladys and Leo's headstone, I found it located in the Arlington Memorial Cemetery in Sacramento, California. It reads as follows:

Photo from www.BillionGraves.com
Photographer: Denis Ashton

This headstone is remarkable in that no date of death is shown for Leo. The question is: <u>why</u>? Why isn't Leo's date of death recorded on this headstone also? What happened here? The answer, I believe, is found on a completely different headstone in a completely different cemetery in Sacramento. In the Camellia Memorial Lawn Cemetery in Sacramento, which is only around two corners from the Arlington Cemetery, about a 3-minute drive away, is a gravestone which reads as follows:

Photo from www.BillionGraves.com
Photographer: Brock Welch

What happened here? We can only conjecture — but here is my guess:

When Leo married Gladys, his family members must have been highly opposed to the union. After all, how could this man they loved marry a woman of pure evil? She had been married 7 times before, and she had been convicted of 1st degree murder for conspiring in the death of her 6th husband. How could Leo be so foolish? How could he make such a terrible decision?

But Leo didn't care. He was in love! And he was bound and determined to marry this woman of his dreams. And by all appearances it must have been a good marriage after all. They remained married for 12 years until Gladys died on August 14, 1973. This made her final marriage, by far, the longest Gladys was married to anyone. And when she died, Leo still cared deeply for her, and he buried her in the Arlington Memorial Cemetery, fully intending that when he died, he would be buried beside Gladys. And he placed a headstone over her grave showing those intentions.

But his family was still furious, even after the 12 years of his marriage to Gladys and the subsequent 12 years after her death. So, when Leo died in 1985, his family put their foot down. "Nothing doing — not a chance!" was their attitude toward the situation. There was no way they were going to bury this man they loved beside that embodiment of evil. So, despite his wishes, they buried Leo in a completely different cemetery, ensuring he would not be linked to a murderess for eternity.

EPILOGUE 3 – THE POINSETTIA BOX

My father, Martin P. Gallagher (known as "Buck"), was also an attorney and he and my grandfather, P.J. Gallagher, were partners in Ontario. My dad was a member of the Oregon State Legislature in 1946, so he was unavailable to assist in the trial of Gladys Broadhurst. When Buck died in 1980, I inherited a family trunk full of photos, letters and other family memorabilia. This trunk (actually a half trunk, only about half as long as a typical steamer trunk) had originally belonged to my grandparents and was passed on to Dad when his parents died. And when Dad died, I inherited the trunk.

I have toted this trunk with me every time I moved in the 30 years or more since I inherited it. I've only gone through it a few times, and I have never taken the time to read everything in it. However, in the bottom of that trunk was discovered a 10" x 10" x 3" deep pasteboard box decorated all over with poinsettia flowers. This was indeed the box that Gladys took from the Caldwell ranch on October 22, 1946, which she handed to her attorney Cleve Groome when Sheriff Moline threatened to confiscate it.

The box contained a number of letters from Doctor Broadhurst to Gladys, many of them sent during Gladys and Alvin's trip to California. All of these letters are included below. There were also several other documents of interest that also are included below. Beyond that were some miscellaneous financial documents of little interest, which are not included in this book.

This box and its contents were never located by the prosecution and unavailable to them for the trial. I presume it has been in this trunk since the trial began, and I am quite certain no one has read these letters since that time until now. Perhaps the prosecution would have been very excited to see these letters and documents and use them in the trial, but they achieved the outcome of the trial they wanted, and they obtained a just verdict.

Since neither Willis Broadhurst nor Gladys had any children, I believe it is appropriate to include these letters in this book.

EPILOGUE 4 – LATER ENCOUNTERS

The story of the murder and the subsequent trial of Gladys Broadhurst was big news in Oregon and Idaho, particularly in Treasure Valley. The *Ontario Argus* (which was later combined with the *Observer* to become the *Argus Observer*) carried daily updates on the progress of the trial. But the story was sensational enough that it was carried in newspapers across America. Articles about the trial were carried in Boise, Portland and even as far away as Phoenix, Arizona and Baltimore, Maryland. But of course, being really big news in Eastern Oregon and Western Idaho, it was closely followed by everybody.

When I was in the fifth grade, the 1958-1959 school year, our teacher was Mrs. Ogilvie. One time in class, Mrs. Ogilvie made an impassioned speech about the failures of the criminal justice system, and in particular, she castigated the evil attorneys who helped criminals escape the justice they deserved. I'm not quite sure how it became apparent, but clearly, I knew that the comments were directed in particular to me. I felt like I was in trouble, but for years I didn't understand what this was all about.

It wasn't until working on this book that I began to understand the background of Mrs. Ogilvie's comments. Her maiden name was Marie Oakes, and she was the daughter of Ed Oakes, who had been the foreman of the jury that convicted Gladys of murder in the first degree. She was 23 years old at the time of the trial and no doubt heard her father discuss the trial many times at the dinner table. And when Gladys was paroled from her "life sentence" in 1957, no doubt she and her father and her whole family had many discussions about this and felt as did many in the community that justice had been perverted. After all, 9 years doesn't come close to "life."

Therefore, just a year or so later, when she had in her class the grandson of the hated attorney who helped make a travesty of justice for this wicked woman, she just couldn't control the urge to make it known how she felt about the situation. But at the tender age of 12, I had no clue what she was talking about. I just knew it wasn't good for me!

A similar but kinder situation occurred later in life. As an adult, I had become a member of the Church of Christ in Ferndale, Washington. When I visited my father, I would attend the friendly congregation in Ontario and became friends with a number of the members there. Once I was invited to join in on a "potluck lunch," which is always very enjoyable. The lunch was hosted in the home of one of the key members of the congregation, Earl Flock, who was an older gentleman at the time, and his wife. He made the comment to me, "I can't believe Pat Gallagher's grandson is a member of the church!" I took it that he never thought an Irish Catholic boy would ever become a member of the Church of Christ.

It was years later, when working on this book, that I learned that Earl Flock had also been a member of the jury for Gladys Broadhurst's trial. Oh, how I wish I had realized it then and asked him a whole host of questions!

APPENDIX 1 – LETTERS

The initial wire from Gladys to the Doctor is not authentic. (Likewise, its twin sent to Leo). It was created by the author to fit the facts from W.D.'s response dated September 5th:

```
TAFT, CAL  20 AUGUST 1945  1330 HRS
TO: W.D. BROADHURST, CALDWELL, IDAHO
VIA: WESTERN UNION

DEAREST BROADY: MEMORIES OF OUR
NIGHTS TOGETHER SO MANY YEARS AGO
STILL FLOOD MY DREAMS TODAY. STOP. I
HAVE NEVER FORGOTTEN YOU. STOP. HOW
COULD I EVER FORGET A MAN LIKE YOU?
STOP.
I'D LOVE TO TELL YOU MY STORY. STOP.
PLEASE WRITE WITH YOUR ADDRESS IF
INTERESTED:
     GLADYS RALPHS LINCOLN
     411 S 7 ST
     TAFT, CA

STOP.
```

The following letter is the doctor's response to Gladys' initial wire:

DR. W. D. BROADHURST

Drugless Physician

THE IDAHO FIRST NATIONAL BUILDING
CALDWELL, IDAHO

Sept. 5, 1945.

Mrs. Gladys Ralphs Lincoln,
Taft, Calif.

Dear Gladys:

Just arrived home form a vacation and found
your telegram awaiting me, so I hurry to answer it and
state that there is no Mrs. - hence no children. As to
any other heirs, I have none. -

An anxiously awaiting a letter giving me all
the details of your past, present and future. Especially
anxious to learn about your folks as I always thot much
of them. Can imagine many things, but one never knows
until someone tells the details. Anyway am hoping for a
favorable report.

Had hoped to be out of practice before now,
but the war came along and took my nephew who was going to
take over so now I have been stuck for a long time and
if nothing happens I am hoping that he will be released
from overseas this fall. Guess I'll have to stay with him
for a year or so and then I am going to take the balance
of my life in the open fooling around with the ranches and
doing the many things I have always wanted to do.

Happy for all that the war seems to be over
and that peace my reign againin the near future. Never
was much of a person for trouble and so I have lived a
life very free from it. Naturally had my little disappointments but it had never made me bitter or sour on the world
in general. Brighter days are always in storeand so I live
every day the best I know how.

Could ask a million questions but am hoping
you will write thereby answering many that I'll not need
to answer. Better get hold of yourself and get that health
that all should have.

Getting busy so shall have to run along and until I hear, I am

Sincerely,

W. D. Broadhurst

"Brody"

The letter from Gladys dated 9/10/1945, shown below
is not authentic. It is the author's creation, attempting to

embody Gladys' questions in her effort to encourage W.D.'s interest yet avoid raising red flags.

September 10, 1945
My Dear Darling Doctor Broady:
    I recall with great fondness the time we spent together so many years ago. I have never forgotten you… how could I ever forget you? I am sure you have had a good life with health and happiness. Unfortunately for me, I am a widow with no children.
    I hope you are well. As for me, my health is still not so good and I miss having someone like you to talk things over. If you are interested, I will be happy to write, sharing with you how my life has been since we parted.
    There is absolutely no doubt in my mind that you saved my life when you treated me back in Burley almost 20 years ago, Doc. Had it not been for your great skill as a chiropractor, coupled with your deep kindness, I surely would have taken my own life then, or it would have slipped away from me of its own accord. There is no understanding the depths of despair a human being can reach, or how insurmountable is the climb out of such a pit. Yet, you were there and like an angel you reached down and lifted me out of the depths.
    I have had much good fortune of late, and I would like to share in that with you, due to my deep gratitude for what you have meant to me. My dearly beloved Aunt Mary from Honolulu has

recently passed away and left her wonderful fortune to me, almost three million dollars. As it is more than I have ever dreamed of owning, and more than I could possibly manage, I have determined to share a small portion with those in my life who have meant the most. I would like to provide a small gift to you. If you would like that, I will instruct my attorney to include you in the disbursement. Due to the size of the estate, I have been advised it will be some time before the legal requirements are finalized.

Please do write and let me know how you have been.

With enduring love,
Gladys

This Christmas card is undated but must have been sent for Christmas 1945.

Addressed to: Gladys Elaine Lincoln
My Dear,

The little package I am mailing you is very much to my liking & am hoping it is not duplicating anything you have. Really do not know your likes & dislikes, but since women have advanced to larger handbags thot you might like its quality.

Trusting health is rapidly coming your way & that soon you will have gained it,

I am,
Your Dr. "Broady"

This undated letter is guessed to have been an early one from W.D. to Gladys. The author suggests a date of 3/10/46. This letter is exceptional for seeing the relationship from the Doctor's eyes:

```
Letterhead:Dr. W. D. BROADHURST
Drugless Physician
THE IDAHO FIRST NATIONAL BUILDING
CALDWELL, IDAHO
```

Monday

Honey Darling:
    Thunder, lightning & rain really tore the earth up around here last nite & as a consequence today has been extremely cool - one needed his flannels regardless of color.
    Made arrangements to take a prospective buyer for stock ranch in Thursday a.m. & we will possibly be gone all day. However, he wants to buy on contract, but being one of the good Mormon boys & being very successful in all his business pursuits, I shouldn't feel badly if I had to sell on contract. Also have another fellow on the string. May be a busy for a time.
    Many, many years ago in the wilds of Idaho there was born to a happy father & mother a cute little baby girl. Being a much wanted child she flourished and grew & was the joy of all the household.
    School days came & she & brothers trudged thru sagebrush amidst coyotes, & jackrabbits, until she was quite a young lady. Being of a temperamental

nature she loved music & later became the pianist of a five man band, playing for dances & other various occasions.

Later a young professional man came to town & her folks hearing about him brot two of the family to see him, she included. Being attractive & full of the girlhood goodness she talked to this young Dr. with ease & gracefulness during the time of their professional calls. Somehow attracted by like vibrations their two souls seemed doomed to vibrate together & agreeably they began to see much of each other. For a short time they were parted & then like lightning they met again & so their love endured, grew & flourished & often had it not have been disturbed by the Mothers possibly would have perpetuated itself in those early days.

Being a girl of honor she kept her promise to a dying uncle & so for the time this beautiful love drifted apart both broken hearted. Miles and years separated them only in person for deep in the hidden realms of human vibrations two hearts beat as one. Two years later she called to see the Dr. who had moved to another town. This time a backache had placed itself well in the mind & only seeing the Dr. could relieve such a pain. Again she was spurred on by the childhood love & could right contacts have been made she would have gladly given all to have realized her deep glory.

Fate was cruel & so, years, & years passed & not to often a brief message exchanged only as a signal that life was not complete & true love had never been found again. Both worked hard & both lonesome for which both had longed & almost died for.

War came & loved ones were snatched away much as a chicken grabs a worm. She became ill & still no solution to a lost loved one. Finally courage bolstered the modest little lady to again try to find that which had been parted but not lost & so telegrams came, finally letters, with much explanation & regret. Like a star from Heaven the flame was kindled anew & so in her modest yet humble way she gave a life's proposal & only too glad the other lonely lover accepted.

Fate had been very unfair & unkind to this Darling & so she had fallen in spirits to those who wanted material wealth & cared not how it was gained. At the lowest ebbtide she was snatched again into the arms of her loved one & shown how cruel & unscrupulous beasts can be in their desire for wealth unearned.

Doped unnatural sleep was replaced by confidence, love & the right way of life & on that she breathed a new heritage – homes, & all she had yearned & prayed for became a reality. In a few weeks roses & strawberries bloomed in the lips & cheeks of what had been a bleached sheet. Life was born anew.

Still troubled from past abuses & wanting to settle all her past affairs with her unscrupulous pursuers, she left in body only & with a vibrant promise that when the score was settled & fear was conquered she would & could return a free soul to love cherish, & live life at will with the one who thru 20 years was devoted. May life mean as much & more as our love has echoed times without number thru the many lonely years.

Now with a solidity of purpose, a love undreamed of may life hold every dream, wish, hope & desire & may we always be free & open to discuss at will anything that materially affects our love.

Darling this is my prayer & I hope you will enjoy it with me as it is just as I feel. My love for you is the finest & I fully realize mine could never be that way for you if it didn't have the exact complement in you. With our years of unhappiness we should have profited much & now realize what a blessing it is to have love, wealth & all the blessings for a united life unto eternity.

Hope your cold is much better & that all is well again.

In closing, please write often as your fine letters mean so much.

Mommie Dear I love you so much.

Your Darling Daddie

Five days after their marriage, shortly after W.D. returned to Caldwell, he sent this letter to Gladys. It was used by the prosecution as evidence in the trial. It became known as the "that brute" letter.

Undated Letter

Letterhead:Dr. W. D. BROADHURST
Drugless Physician
THE IDAHO FIRST NATIONAL BUILDING
CALDWELL, IDAHO

Sat.

Dearest Wifie,

So happy to get my first letter from you on Thurs. as I was uneasy about your safety. While at sisters I had a dream & I told her that things weren't going so well with you & I'd bet you had had another mixup with that brute. However, while on the subject of sister did she ever write you? I told her all about us & our marriage & she said she was writing you. She was very happy to think we had gotten together but very sorry about your state of health & trouble. She is one mum sister.

The big roundup starts June 15th & I'll not be in or around Jordan until about July 1st, so hardly know how I'll stand not hearing a word from you, cause I am very much in love with my Dear little Momma. Did I ever tell you I love you? Nope, never heard the word, just caught your vibrations. Darn my Daddy he does love me

Honey did you get the hundred dollar P.O. money order? Hope so. Now I'll mail you another $200 today & I want you to get out of that town. I had thot you could go to Long Beach down to your cousin's for a time & surely you could find a room eventually there. Now pack what you have, leave no forwarding adds., buy your ticket part way & then re-buy another. By no means leave any clue as to your whereabouts & by no means have any correspondence to Sac. Why not Daddy? Nobody talks if they know nothing, & no pressure can be brot to make them talk. Give them the slip until I can get some place for us to live. Better get out as soon as possible.

Now as to your bills for Dr. & etc., find out how much & see if they will be O.K. until I can get something sold, then I'll be able to meet them. Better get going immediately Honey as we need each other & no lunatic like that guy can stop us. Certainly wouldn't tell Pete or the Mrs. – NOBODY.

Now these are only my suggestions & not demands so do the best you think possible, but please Honey get away from there.

You can find good respectable Drs. To give you the shots & get away from all that fear which will mean a lot, besides a change in climatic conditions. As soon as I return I'll try to send you more money.

Honey Sweet, for gosh sake buy yourself some clothes as you certainly need not go around in tatters. Clothes certainly don't make the man, but they help the appearance a lot & you can be so darn cute when you really fix up. Naturally, I know how you feel, no pep & no ambition to do anything, but one can never allow themselves to drift into a no-care attitude cause just see how much we have to live for. Daddy loves you in tatters, but he is so proud of his little spick & span Mrs. Also. What will you do for me? "Anything humanly possible, Dear." O.K., listen to husband.

Now I am just talking Honey & that is who is going to make our lives heavenly for I know you are of my very heart & soul – Talk things over, discuss everything & then do the best for the most concerned. Right? I do love you, your prince does.

Needless to say our first nite was heavenly & to think of the more heavenly things to come when you are well & all worries obliterated & peace reigns for us again. I'll do my best in every way possible to make you happy & I in turn will be happy too. Gosh I'll bet you tease me for some more – Candy.

Do not suppose I'll get another chance to write before I leave, but want you to get away as soon as possible. Change add. At P.O. & not allow any mail to go out to 2228 ½ H St. Should have been a detective. I wonder if I could get Sac. To deputize me this fall & I'll get that dirty Brute.

Must run so until later I am,
Your loving
Broady Husband

About three weeks after their marriage, W.D. sent the following letter. Obviously, Leslie Lincoln had intercepted one of W.D.'s letters and learned his wife had committed bigamy. This letter is an amazing window into the mind of Doctor Broadhurst. When faced with compelling information that his new wife may be less than honest, he dismisses it with a presumption of innocence on her part.

```
Mailed via: Air Mail
Mailed to: Gladys Broadhurst
c/o Big Chief Camp
Box 625
Truckee, CA

Note: hand-written in pencil on the
back of the envelope: "Aunt Lillie,
Box 206"
Postmark:Boise, ID - Sep 15, 1946
```

Also note: the letter says "Monday" at the top (with no date) but it was found in an envelope dated 9/15/46, which is a Sunday. I have dated this letter 6/10/46, as it fits well here and may perhaps have been placed in the wrong envelope.

```
Letterhead:Dr. W. D. BROADHURST
Drugless Physician
THE IDAHO FIRST NATIONAL BUILDING
CALDWELL, IDAHO

Monday

My Dearest Wifie:
     Well a reign of terror started
in Caldwell yesterday as Dr. & I were
away when the telephone rang & Lola
answered & Sac. was calling. She told
them we would be back around 6 P.M.
About 9 P.M. the telephone rang & it
```

was Sac. again. The voice was that of a Mr. Lincoln, so he said, & he was your husband. He stated that he was at your place when my telegram came yesterday a.m. (Sunday) & that you had told him you had gone to Reno May 20th to see your brother. He also went on to state that you, meaning me, married Gladys Ralphs Lincoln on May 20 in Reno & I told him that was right. However, I also stated in reply to his statement that this complicated matters much as I did not know that you had a living husband at the time we were married. Imagine my surprise, according to his statement, to think that I have a wife & do not have one. Well Honey I haven't let it worry me to much & am not for I could never feature you doing such, inhuman, illegal, uncivilized acts of behavior.

However, I was surprised to think that he had gotten hold of the telegram & knew its contents, if he did. I surely hope he doesn't get hold of the airmail letter today with the $200 P.O. office money order. Possibly he has gotten many of my letters. Did you get the other $100 I sent you? Needless to say, he stated he didn't want anymore to do with you.

What kind of a gangdom do you have down there Honey? My god it must be terrible.

I told him there wasn't much I could do about it as I was ignorant of the fact you were still married. He said he thot I did everything innocently. I thanked him & stated I should have to wait for something to happen for you certainly couldn't be married legally to both of us.

Naturally I still believe you are my lawfully, legally wedded wife & that you were right in everything you said or did. So I am not heeding any warning until such time as you advise me personally. Gosh I know you could not or would not willfully do anything in the world to mar & interfere with prospective future. After 20 years of yearning & longing to be brot to a climax by marrying each other - I trust we may continue the long stretch ahead with all the joy & happiness endowed in human souls.

Naturally I couldn't see how someone killed in a rade in England, reported dead, - Gov't paying ins., could be reserected & come to be a living human being interested in letting me know you were his legal wife. My amazement was beyond the human mind to fathom & still is.

Sorry I am going to be gone for two weeks as I'll worry much about you & your safety. Myself I have no fear but with this strange Lincoln man calling me, I hardly know what to do. Must go on the roundup as it is an absolute necessity otherwise I think I should be down there. As soon as I get back from there then we start haying & that is a month or 6 weeks. Gosh if I only knew everything & could contact you hourly, I could rest at ease.

Well Honey give me the lowdown
& if I am not your lawful wedded
husband, which I do not question but
what I am, I'll make out somehow. Gosh
such a mess as we human beings have
to endure.

Darling you are the only one
in whom I have all the faith and
confidence in the world. I have no
doubt as to your legal rights or that
you are entirely in the clear, & that
all will be O.K., but I should like to
hear what that Mr. Lincoln told you.

So long Darling until I return from
the roundup & take care of yourself.
I love you & trust everything will be
100%.

Your loving husband
Broady

Having totally rejected the possibility that Gladys
could be guilty of what he terms an "inhuman, illegal and
uncivilized" act, W.D. leaves for the scheduled roundup.

When things go from bad to worse in Sacramento for
Gladys, she panics and sends the following letter to Floyd
only 10 days later:

Tell Broady to drive down
as he will need the car.

Sac. Calif
June 20/4

Dear Dr. Adams + Family:
am most pleased to meet
you if only by phone etc. Dr
Broddy has told me so much
about you folks I almost
ful I know you already.
　　　　Doc. I have a serious
Problem, I must get word to
my husband, Dr. Broady at
once; that I am seriously
ill with blood poisoning in
my left leg + before the decision
is made to take off said foot
I feel that my husband Dr.
Broady) should be here to

S.M.

say "yes" or "no". I feel he
would say no, but regardless
Doc. Please please Contact
Dr. Broady + tell him to come
as quickly as he can. I know
he is busy + on roundup,
but if I die he wouldn't
be able to stand it. We sincerely
love each other. He + I only
had three short days together.
We were so happy. He has been
sending me some money, but
its him I need. I just have
a room here + the folks have
asked me to move or at least
have my husband come to
my rescue. Have a brother

3. ✓

in F. B. I. but they wont tell me
where he is, I imagine over seas
he is under gov. ardees + isint
allowed to disclose his whereabouts.
        Please sence the scriffle
I dont usually write so badly
but I've had no food for 5 days
+ am in terrible pain - you
cant buy butter eggs meat
bread + very few clothes, I surely
never want to see calif again
        Did Dr. Brady tell you
about my aunt mary Ralpho
Johnson who died last august
in Honlulu T.H. She left Dr +
I nearly three Million dollars,
Plus my own desarted Parents.

4' estate now in probation. The
Hawaiian estate will be thru
Probation about 1st of the year, so
you can see Brody need not
work his self to death. Course
I always want him to do the things
which will make him happy & I
know he enjoys the cattle, I do too
but right now, you will have to
make him see I need him at
once. Otherwise I would not
change any of his plans for
the world, but I'm about to
die doe, & am pleading with
you to find Mr. Brody, &
inform him of the Truth, I
think he loves me enough to

Come to me in my desperate plight.

Broady knew. I was thin & run down & I expect he wanted me to stay here till fall + take liver + B1. shots, Had built up late, but I stepped on a rusty nail + it didn't take much to undo all the building up process

I know you will do your best to tell him what has happened. — Tell him to drop every thing + bring what summer clothes he has, My rent is paid here till July 15th, However the main issue is its a matter of Life or death with me, Dr. Engelberg was out this a:m: + dressed my leg

6.

He said, "you better get in touch with your husband, you arent doing so good." I said I didnt know where he was, so will have to leave that up to you to find him + tell him to come.

I'm sorry I have to bother you, as Mr. B. had meant to keep his marriage a secret. He told sister Sarah Allen + she wrote me a long letter.

Please dont fail me

Love to all.

phone
27452.

Gladys Ralph Broadhurst
2288½ H Street
Sacramento Calif

P. S.

Sent letter + wire 19th Travelers aide sent wire to day.

I spent three years in Service too. Army nurse. 1st. Lt. never went over seas but they surely kepted us busy. Had all four brothers + myself in. my baby brother was killed + one last in France. He was found alive but had amnesia due to head injury. Steil the other brother was in plane crash, + is in Vets hospital in L.A. Jess my eldest brother is Capt. in F.B.I. So we know   S.M.

there was a war as we were all in it. I dont think Sterl will ever be able to walk much as his legs are still in casts.

— The air mail letter I sent Broady is very important because it contains our marriage certificate. I tried to keep it a secret but he wrote me as Gladys Ralphs Broadhurst & Sister Sarah same so most everyone I know here knows. It wasnt because either he or I were ashamed, just that he had no house + he wanted to wait till fall. The rest I'll leave to you Dr. Adams - Please -

Love Gladys.

W.D. wrote to Gladys on August 7, 1946, two days after Gladys & Alvin depart for California:

Postmark dated: Aug 7, 1946 - Boise, Idaho and also Aug. 8, 1946 - Truckee Cal
Addressed to: Mrs. Gladys Broadhurst, c/o Big Chief Lodge, Sterling Ralphs, Truckee, CA

Registered Mail
Hotel Owyhee
C. F. MANN, MANAGER
Boise, Idaho

Wed. a.m.
My Dearest Beloved Wifie:
     Have I ever told you I love you? Well here goes, as I am madly in love with you & miss you more than anything in the world. Thot it bad enuf to be away from you for a few hours, but now days & weeks creep into the picture it is terrible. Hardly know how to tell you how much I miss you & love you but a little imagination will get very close to the answer.
     Disked two days & came down last nite - rose early yesterday 4 a.m., & went to work cause I didn't have any Momma in bed with me. Came in for breakfast about 6:30 & then ate no lunch as I wanted to finish.
     Dr. & Lola feeling much better & had a nice talk with them about things in general. Lola stated her actions were caused from her being sick & not from any unkind feeling toward us as she loved us both very

much. I feel certain that they got my point of view & know exactly how we feel about the whole setup.

George Vogt, our neighbor next door north had a birthday last nite & since they had a loudspeaker & yard all lighted we listened to the program from the steps of home enjoyed it very much. Mommie I love you.

Today I came to Boise to bring some side boards to uncle Billie, list the stock ranch, see Mr. Cranston, the Grocery Dept. & incidentally obtain a birth certificate. Guess I was never born for they have no record earlier than 1911. Was I born or was I just kidded into this old world? Anyway I have the form to fill out to be sent to Mrs. Adams for an affidavit & then I'll know if I were born.

Honey I am enclosing $100 bill for you & since I left the add. On the box am taking a big chance on you getting this. However, I'll register it so I'll be certain that it does not go astray.

If only I could hold you in my arms & tell you I love you for just a moment how happy I should be. Not long until I do I hope. I am so terribly lonesome & then Bernard being gone next week will make it worse. Gosh such a silly Daddy.

Have on my light trousers, green silk shirt & blue famous brands tie - already for the rodeo tonite. Wish my darling were here to be with cause we could have so much fun.

> Hope you are getting along fine &
> that you know I am thinking about you
> every second & loving you so much.
>   To be hearing real soon & to be
> seeing you sooner, I am
>   Your most loving
>   Dr. Husband
>
> (Written on the side of the last
> page): Think I'll go to Jordan
> tomorrow.

This letter was found in the box of trial documents in Salem. It had been torn up and was later taped back together. Obviously, this letter was one of the documents retrieved by the sheriff from the heat duct in Gladys' room at the house. Written at the top in another handwriting: "**10-30-46 #3**" plus two sets of initials, WSW and CG

> Postmark: Truckee, CA 8/8/46
> Big Chief, Cal
>
> Darling, Darling, Darling,
>   I miss you, I love you. How much
> is as the vastness of the blue blue
> sky here. Forgive me honey please for
> not wanting you to come at this time,
> it's so beautiful here, it hurts
> one's eyes. Al is overwhelmed. He's
> speechless. He wants to stay here. He
> is opening shingles for Tony. He drove
> very well, but it was so hot we nearly
> died. Will come back in the night.
> We got a parking ticket at Reno one
> peso. Never did find out why??
>   I go to court Monday 10 P X -
> going before another judge - would
> have gone yesterday, but Tony is ill.

Has been working too hard. We played together the other night & really had a time so spects he is tired. He was so happy to see me he cried. He looks fine tho, but stomach is haywire. Needs a course with my daddy. They were amazed how good I looked. Had my hair fixed nice at Reno, & so mommie just looked her best for her brother.

How I appreciate you darling. I know how hard it was to let me go, but soon we can go together always.

Don't work too hard darling. I miss you at nite always snuggling up to my honey – it's cold here and no daddy.

Will write again tomorrow Darling. Helping Gwynie today. Help is short. Write me here precious. I love you, I adore you, my darling nite dearest man in the world.

Love from us all
Your lil mommie wife

Big Chief Camp
Box 625
Truckee, Calif

Willis wrote to Gladys on August 8th:

Mailed via: Air Mail
Mailed to: Gladys Broadhurst
c/o Sterling Ralphs
Big Chief Lodge
Truckee, CA

Postmark:Caldwell, ID – Aug 9, 1946
Letterhead:Dr. W. D. BROADHURST
Drugless Physician

THE IDAHO FIRST NATIONAL BUILDING
CALDWELL, IDAHO

Thursday

My Darling Beloved Baby:
     Needless to say, I love you & miss
you a lot more than this pen & words
can tell so just remember that your
Daddy is a very lonesome, lonesome
man. Why? Cause my Momma is just to
darn far away. Never, never again are
you going to get away from him even if
he has to tag along where not wanted.
Guess I am a baby, but I'll candidly
admit for you I am more than that.
Love love you so much.
     Dr., Lola, the kids & I went to
the Rodeo last nite & enjoyed it much
only thing wrong I had no Momma to
help me enjoy it.
     The announcer was giving the
history of a particular ride & in so
doing he stated this man had quite a
rear & then realized his slip & added
career. The crowd just hooted. Much
difference I should say. Well it was
funny anyway.
     Parade, bucking horses, calf
roping, Brahma bulls, bull-dogging &
all were good & so we all had a good
time.
     Have tried to work in the yard
today but it has been allowed to
run down so much that I made little
headway. Must go back to Jordan early
tomorrow as Bernard wants to get away
tomorrow.

Now your Dr. Daddy will be there all alone, but if I can find enuf work & get tired enuf I'll try to console myself until you arrive. Wish I could hold you in my arms & tell you I love you, adore you & miss you so much. Believe me Momma?

Have the stock ranch listed in several places, & also listed the home ranch just as a feeler. The realtor said he thot he could get $300 per acre for this place & I told him if he could to hop to it, so we might be out of a home some of these days. May be sorry, but I am tired of work.

The flowers are beautiful & as soon as cooler weather comes they are twice as gorgeous. I certainly think the flower garden adds much to the looks of the home.

Figured out the grocery bill, Fay's expenses, meat & the groceries I took in & the cost to me not including milk ran just about $1.00 per meal. Terrible to say the least & if only she could understand what that means in dollars & cents, possibly she could or would try to change her ways.

Was amused the other day while Alice was taking butter & catsup. Fay told her that they cost a lot of money & she was not to waste them so Alice was cut about 2/3 normal waste. I was happy to think that possibly you had given her an inkling of what such wasteful habits meant.

Gosh Momma I'd give a million to see you & talk with you & especially to hold you in my arms. You just wait for you have a lot of lost loving to be made up. I'll not forget.

To be hearing soon & with all my love to my Darling Momma,

Your loving Dr. Daddy, Broady husband

W.D. to Gladys, August 11th:

Envelope postmarked from Jordan Valley, probably Aug. 12, 1946 (exact day not real clear)
Via Air Mail
From: Dr. W. D. Broadhurst
Jordan Valley, Oregon

To:Mrs. Gladys Broadhurst
c/o Big Chief Camp
Box 625
Truckee, Calif

Sunday

My Darling Wifie:

Thanks a million for the fine letter awaiting the one that is supposed to arrive tomorrow. Gosh Darling that letter surely eased an uneasy spot in my heart for it was bleeding big big drops for some kind of appeasement. Why should all this be true, but I can answer in just 3 words, I love you.

Yep the most in the world, I love you & adore you a million times more than I ever dreamed possible. My Momma I miss you so much.

I came to Jordan early Friday, in fact left hrs. before Dr. & Lola thot about getting up. Was to the old ranch just about the time the Turners had breakfast.

I didn't go to the rodeo Thursday evening as I had worked hard so stayed with the kids. Trina was adorable as she was the sweetest little darling about going to bed. O.K. Doc & then a great big hug & kiss & a goodnite.

Helped Bernard finish the hay corrals Friday a.m. & they left early in the afternoon. I rode disc until late & then came in, milked the cow, fed chickens, pigs & then proceeded to try to find heads or tails of the refrigerator. Of all the mushy junk & a thousand dishes instead of one she had them. Anyway outside of 40 dishes with jam in them I have it very much in order. By the way, I have a great big watermelon in there & no one to eat it but me. Gosh how I long for my Momma to be here to help me eat some of this good food.

Harrowed & disked yesterday & if I get up early enuf I'll finish tomorrow, other than drilling & that will have to be completed later as I do not have the seed.

However, have a lot of riding to do this week, gates to fix & a thousand odd jobs. Should you come home & I do not happen to be here, I'll be back in the evening as I have the cow to milk & chores to do. With the many things I think you had to do in Calif. I little look for you for another week. Bernard and Fay should be home a week from today.

Never find time to cook & have not made a fire since they left. Poached some eggs on the hotplate this a.m. & other than that have done no cooking.

Am happy that you were able to go & that Al is amazed with the glory of the outside world. Naturally I am terribly lonesome for My Momma, but happy that your wishes could be filled, even

tho you will never know my grief in parting from you.

Honey believe me now & forever I do not want to appear rude or ugly, but for my life I

can not understand the schrouded secrecy. Naturally I'll never inquire into your business only as you choose to tell me. Sorry, very sorry if I appeared somewhat curious. Forgive me Momma for I love you.

You have mail here & was going to forward it to you, but Fay said for me to not do it as you told her to keep it for her.

Today has been sultry & hot until a dust storm came up & now everything is filled with dust to the brim. Guess I'll have to clean hous as well as the tent.

Gosh Momma while discing & harrowing there is just a cloud of dust & your Daddy comes in the dirtiest blackest man you ever saw. Did you know you married a colored man? Yeps caught you asleep for once & see what you got - a fine big Darkie.

Had a fine big boil in my ear & did I have an earache for a day - broke

last nite & other than sore is O.K.
Think it was caused from a little
sliver obtained while haying.
     Well Darling must go get the cows
as it is nearing that time. So much
good milk & cream that the pigs are
living fat.
     Honey Darling I miss you, love
you & shall be a very happy happy boy
when I can kiss & love you again. Love
to all & all my love to My Darling
Momma.

     Your Dr. Broady man

On the back of the envelope for the above letter, Gladys
has written the office and home phone numbers of two
attorneys. One is for Irvin Ford, who is Leslie's attorney and
the other is D. D. DeCoe, Gladys' attorney in Sacramento.

This next letter was found in the box of trial documents in
Salem. It had been torn up and was later taped back together.
Obviously, this letter was one of the documents retrieved by
the sheriff from the heat duct in Gladys' room at the house.
Written at the top in another handwriting: "**10-30-46 #2**"
plus two sets of initials, Sheriffs WSW and CG

Postmark: Truckee, CA 8/15/46
Big Chief
Truckee

Daddy Darling:
     I'm sorry I couldn't write
yesterday, but just about everything
happened, Tony got sick and we had to
put him to bed, too much overdoing.
It's their rush season & they are
so busy. Gwyn needed help so Allen
helped her & I took care of Tony. Pat

has blood poison in her hand so your lil Mommie nurse had two patients both better today. Now hold your hat honey, I'm going to be an auntie & you uncle Doc, as Gwyn & Tony are going to have a little one, they are wild with joy, me too – I'm scared tho cause Gwyn is working too hard we would all die if she loses it. They have lost one – I try to make her rest. She isn't very strong but God how I envy her. My darling I miss you so & if you were here I would love you to death (X O). Now another big surprise, Jess is in Reno. Haven't seen him yet but he talked to me on the phone. He is on terminal leave We hope. We don't know where Red is yet or Jackie.

The main issue now is getting Tony up again & getting Gwyn to rest a little. They are coming up this fall if all goes well. I'll see Jess Monday at the trial. He says where is that big fat rascal (meaning you).

Darling, why haven't you written? Are you mad at me? I love you & while we don't always see eye to eye we are still completely in love. The best there is, I'm so happy with you but I'll be so glad to be with you when you don't have to work so hard.

I'll be writing again & do hope to hear from you soon. Please honey, take care of yourself. Your lonely Mommie.

X O X O X By

Allen is doing some carpenter work

for Tony.

The letter below is from Willis to Gladys, August 15th:

Envelope postmarked from Jordan
Valley, probably Aug. 15, 1946
(exact day not real clear)
Via Air Mail
From: Dr. W. D. Broadhurst
Jordan Valley, Oregon

To: Gladys Broadhurst
c/o Big Chief Camp
Box 625
Truckee, Calif

Thursday 15 - 46

My Darling Dearest Mommie:
      So happy to get your second letter
today & sorry you had not received
any of mine. However, one was written
Wed. after you left enclosing a $100
P.O. money order, which I know you
rec'd cause I rec'd the return card.
Needless to say it was rec'd by Mrs.
S. A. Ralphs Aug. 12. Now another was
written Thursday and another last
Sunday so you should have rec'd all
by now. A card was sent to Sac. The
same date of the money order. Now how
is that? However, to date you should
have rec'd three more than I have
rec'd.
      Terribly MAD & if you were here,
so I could prove it to you, I would
take it all out in giving you one of
the greatest lovings of all times.
Such a Momma with everything Daddy

loves & yet all I can do is hope, pray & imagine how I should love to have you in my arms to pet & love you as we both love so much. No Darling I have no thot of anger & if you do not receive letters as often as you should like, remember the many things to be done during the course of the day, especially being alone.

Have all the ground ready for fall barley, one & ½ days of riding, one day fixing a gate just east of the house, cemented posts & really hung it in grand style. While speaking of riding rode the Cow Creek country yesterday & found four of our cattle.

Today I went to Caldwell to get gasoline, weed spray & more primarily to get a check on how the cattle sold at the O.K. sales yard. Not bad but I was offered more here for the steers than they were selling for at the yards. May sell about 50 soon. O.K.?

Darling I never worry about our little misunderstandings & only look at them as a means of a greater understanding. While a child we use to have a list of ditches on the farm & I was quite the irrigator & quite often a dam would wear out & from that break it taught me that the next had to be stronger & so a greater understanding. So it is with our little misinterpretations - just a means of knowing our likes & dislikes.

Naturally everybody has had past experiences & so the history, character & reputations of us all are made - some good & some bad, but all in all I feel we rate above the average in building a reputable history of our lives. I married you for better or for worse, & with a full knowledge that I loved you for what you are & whatever you have or have done in the past, I question not & that is none of my business, for it is the YOU of today I love & it shall always be so. We voluntarily tell the things we want to & resent having histories pried open & made a public book. In all the peoples I have dealt with this is a self evident axiom. True today & always will be.

Of all my experiences with women I would not trade one of your sweet, sweet smiles & kind words for all all of them. Fine women to be certain, but it is My Momma that grappled my heart 20 yrs ago & still has it as spellbound as the cat & the mouse. So worry not My Dear One for a heart given so completely as mine will not change as nite the day but only as the great doer of things decides it is time to part. Mommie I love you so much my heart really aches for you.

To be alone without you is the most difficult thing I have endured since I parted 20 yrs. Ago from you. I know you love me dearly & will soon be home but somehow I just cannot understand why you aren't around to be kissed, loved & ready to go to be. Gosh Momma, how long must this go on?

Going to ride the range tomorrow & Sat. Jack Staples & I are going to spray morning glory on both places his & ours. We use the big cattle spray & haul it around in the pickup. Have two 30 ft. hoses with vapor like nozzles. Guess you have never seen it - it's a honey for grubs & lice. Have a lot of weeds down home so may go down as soon as Bernard gets home.

Have partially figured the food bill & as near as I can figure it, it cost $1.00 per meal per man or $3.00 per day for each man. Fay charged me $6.00 per day. Very expensive I should say.

Have found so many eggs that I have the pantry cluttered, yet we had to buy eggs for

haymen. No justice in giving HANDS things to do unless they are guided in the right way. Thank God it has been a quiet week.

Happy to know of the expected arrival & hope all is O.K. with them. Never worry about her working as that is as necessary as food. Just avoid undue strains & all will be O.K. The finest colts I have ever seen born & with the greatest ease are the ones where their mothers worked. A homely comparison, but a fact.

Glad Jess is home & I hope for good but I guess no such luck.

Give my kindest regards to all & tell them that if I do not die from the loneliness I'll be seeing them sometime. Bed time so My Darling I love you, miss you & need you every moment.

Your lonesome Daddy

(Author's note: in the 14th line, W.D. writes "kissed, loved & ready to go to **be**. Gosh, Momma, how long must this go on?" I checked carefully, and W.D. wrote "be" – he may have been thinking "bed" but he wrote "be".)

W.D. wrote again to Gladys, August 17th:

```
Mailed via air mail
Postmarked: Caldwell, Idaho Aug 19,
1946
From:Dr. W. D. Broadhurst
Jordan Valley
Oregon

Addressed to:Mrs. W. D. Broadhurst
c/o Big Chief Camp
Box 625
Truckee, Calif.

Sat. Nite 17-46
My Dearest Momma:
     Gosh how I wish you were here as
your Daddy needs you so much in every
way. Never realized how lonesome &
forgotten it seems until I have to
stay here all alone day in & out & my
Precious Darling so far away.
     Twenty years ago I knew I had to
depart & leave the scene of so many
happy times & the one I have always
loved, but now to have you gone after
having lived with you for a short
time is worse than ever cause you are
absolutely a part of me. Naturally I
think of you every moment, but still
no Darling to pet & love. I care not
what your business is or how urgent
you are never going without me ahold
```

of your glad rags. Gosh I haven't breathed an easy breath in the two weeks you have been away. Surely I'll not have to endure this loneliness much longer. If you are half as lonely as I, I pity you. I love you a million times more than I ever thot two people could love, & I want you with me every moment of the next 100 or 1000 years – maybe a big, big million. Now how do you like all this Bologna? Hope straight from the shoulder & I am not just woofing.

Jack staples & I sprayed morning glory on his ranch today & lacked about 2 or 3 hours of finishing. Have little idea how long it is going to take on this place. Hope not very long. We used the cattle spray machine & it rides nicely in the back of the pickup. Mix 100 gals at a time so if you want to be soaked just appear round the corner of the pickup next Monday or Tuesday & we will give you the works.

Took Patches & P.U. yesterday afternoon & drove to wagontown right where we dropped into Jordan creek on our way to Silver City. Found a cow, calf & steer & drove them down to the old Cow Creek ranch & put them in the field. Late when I arrived home, but in my search for the milk cow ran across a cow with a fine new calf. Gee, it is a beauty & so perfectly marked. I caught him & loved the little darling. Honey the cattle we have in the field are beautiful & wish you were here to enjoy them with me.

They have been feeding most of the time on the alfalfa patch just above the house.

Sort of looking for Bernard home tomorrow, but he may not get here, as he was having a lot of work done on the car. Anyway I am getting many things done with a million more to do.

Helped a poor old sheep out from a mudhole yesterday as she had ventured too far out for a drink & couldn't make it back. She sank deep, deep into the mire.

Have been no where so not much news, but when you get this letter you should have rec'd five letters. Momma, Dear, I love you so much.

Goodnite Darling - nite nite

Gladys wrote to Willis on August 27th, another letter retrieved from the heat vent and reconstructed:

Postmark: Truckee, CA 8/27/46
Big Chief
Truckee

Darling Daddy Dearest:
Why haven't we received answers to our wires Dearest - Jess, Tony & Red, sent wire asking you to come at least for a few days. I wired you twice, once here and once in Sac. Please darling you need to get away for awhile & it's so gorgeous here. Then Jess may go back soon & we want to have a family Party before he leaves. May not see him again. Would you darling? I know it hurt you beyond words when I left,

but I just had to fight this out alone – I love you, adore you honey & I'm only asking one thing more. Please come for a few days. We are so happy you are a part of us now & there will never be another time so ideal for all of us to be together – I know you are busy, busy but a few days in this spot will take away all your cares. Alvin is wild about it here and wants to stay & cut trees. He has been very nice to me. I'm glad you chose him as he is honest & decent. He is going to ride for Big Chief Camp Sept. 2nd in Rodeo. Please come honey. Take the bus & then Mommie & Daddy can go home together.

Have taken care of all I could for the the present. Will tell you all about it.

Thanks for your letter and the $100.00 you are so good to me. I love you.

I'm fine cept I'm awfully lonesome. I'd never wanted to be away again, but honey I did the thing I wanted & I'm free of fear on that score. Had you helped me, I'd still be weak. Please come & see your surprise. Honey don't fail me. It's about the most important thing in my life to have you meet my family & spend a few days with us. I just can't bear it if you don't come. Please daddy – Sweetheart.

Called Dr. Adams and the only wire you got was the one from Sac. You didn't get the one from the Ralphs Brothers inviting you down. I feel Jess must leave soon so hurry honey.

```
Take the Bus & then call Big Chief
Camp & we will get you at Truckee.

     Bye darling, please don't fail me
 -
     Your loving wife
     Flea X O

Send whatever you feel like in
money, but won't stay here much
longer but would so love a few days
with you here. It's an ideal place
for a few days honeymoon.

     X O X O
```

W.D. to Gladys, the day he departed from Big Chief Camp to return to Caldwell, Sept, 6th. He is lonely and heartbroken, but still is willing to take the blame for the challenges in their relationship. This is a very important letter in understanding the mindset of Willis:

```
Postmark dated: Sept, 7, 1946 - 9 AM
- Winnemucca, Nev.
Addressed to: Gladys Broadhurst, c/o
Big Chief Camp, Box 625, Truckee,
Calif.


Hotel Humboldt
Gus Knezevich, Managing Owner
Winnemucca, Nevada

8 P.M.

My Most Darling Wifie:
     Needless to say I left the most
important part of this old framework
in Big Chief, & altho you may not be
```

able to locate it in houses, tents, cars, rivers & etc. it should be ever present in every movement, act, or thot you think. Possibly not visible to the naked eye, the ears, or the skin, but it is there & in such an abundance that I feel completely lost – possibly I'll recover but slowly. Momma Dear, to me, you are the grandest, dearest, most Divine soul I have ever known. Believe me Dearest, this is as I have always felt, & trust you are as completely sold to our vastness of love as I.

Only as you have peace of mind can I ever hope to, for whatever disturbs you likewise effects me. I can be brave & shout to the hilltops that it doesn't, but I am only kidding the inner man & soon Mr. Conscious gets on the scene & utters in silence, "Man know thyself better, for two hearts that have loved, longed & bleed for each other so long can never be troubled unless both are effected in like manner." Darling this is true as nite the day & rightly so for vibrations travel & are received by those who are in tune to receive them & I know that I am one who is a perfect receiving set for your vibrations.

All I have ever said or done has always been with the greatest feeling & spirit of trying to help you. Wrong in many things & subject to errors & mistakes always but when convinced of these facts, I can admit it frankly & in no way ever feel an unkindly feeling or thot toward My Dearest.

Only as we can do these things can life be worth the living. I love you.

I have known ever since I met you in Feb. that you were ever so troubled & in my humble way have given the best I have. Possibly not always to your liking, but I am only human & have many human weaknesses, but in my SOUL I have every thot of trying to be helpful. That which I do not see & do will be the things & reasons why I could do no more. My heart is still there just the same.

I have my chin up & feet flatly on the floor & can look the whole world in the face & tell them that I love you adore you & worship the very earth around you. I can offer no more & likewise no less, as this completes the cycle that I would do nothing knowingly to detract from that kindred sacredness. And as surely as the sun rises & I see its lite, I am always willing to give you everything in life that my capabilities permit. They may not be all the glamour & fame that some possess, but they will be genuine & as rich as my very life can make them.

Often we are misled by blarney, glittering brightness & our emotions & think how foolish we were to accept anything other than the above mentioned, but still deeper far deeper than the eye can see or the ear hear lies a brilliance that has depth, breadth & a sense of endurance that lasts forever. So it is in my love for you, & I believe with your love as well, it will last until the end of time.

If our time to part should come tomorrow, I could truthfully say that as far as I had known how to help you, I had not failed. However, not knowing many things have taken place, all for which I am truly sorry, but from these I can build & avoid the same mistakes again.

I can see now, after having talked to you & understanding some of your past how easily I could have been more of a hindrance than a help in your liberation of fear & many other troubles. Yet My Dear, until I knew it was that big pioneering heart of your most ardent lover that spoke in challenge to anyone that attempted to harm you. Just my primitive nature protecting his loved one. Forgive Me Darling & forget any unpleasantness that may have come our way. As certainly as I know I hold no grievances or a thot in this wide, wide world other than that one that can be added to make our lives harmonious & beautiful.

Had you been well & without fear & worry, I often wonder, if life would have had more meaning and if thru these trying times the greatest understanding will not come. Never for a moment have I regretted our marriage, otherwise it has given me someone to try to help & I most assuredly hope & pray that my handicaps to you can be far offset by possibly a greater help. Anyway, I hope this is true, most fervently.

Now Darling give my regrets to G. & Tony for not bidding them goodbye this a.m. but I didn't see them & we had very little time to spare. Thank them a million times for their extreme kindness & assure them that in SHIRT & SOUL I love them as tho they were my own.

Leave this lonely town at eleven & arrive in Caldwell 6:25 a.m. Tired & lungs pretty tight but head seems to be draining quite well. Worry not for your Daddy wants to live just to love & help you all his life & I hope that be a long long one.

Momma Dear, I so hope that the continued stay with your folks will be happy, healthful & that when you decide to come home you will do so with a heart full of joy & a feeling & knowledge that your Daddy is lonesome, arms wide open & has a much broader knowledge of how you feel & why so. All I have is yours & I share it with you as freely as I share the greatest love in the world.

Darling I miss you so much & to love you & to know you are present is my life in its entirety.

Nite Darling & please write often to your very lonesome Daddy.

Most & all my love, Daddy.

W.D. to Gladys, September 7th:

DR. W. D. BROADHURST
Drugless Physician
THE IDAHO FIRST NATIONAL BUILDING
CALDWELL, IDAHO

Sat. Afternoon.

My precious Darling Wiffie:

Wrote you a letter last nite when I was tired
and sleepy and told you that the bus was to leave at 11pm
but instead one was late ad so we pulled out at 1230. Thot
the time would never pass but arrived at 6:25 this a.m.
Called Dr. Adams and he came right in and got me. Had a little
breakfast with them and then went back to town with him and
stayed doing the many things i had to do. However, have not
closed my eyes since I lay along side of you Friday a.m. as
the buss was so noisy and cold that I nearly froze to death.
Needless to say I hope to be able to sleep tonite. Just
guess I'll never get use to trying to sleep without MY Darling
Mamma. Darling did I ever tell you that I loved you? Well just
in case I havennever done so I am going to elaborate just a
little and give you a sort of synopsis of just how my inner
feeling click.
First of all I am visualizing a beautiful little
girl about 40, sweet and sincere, honest and good standing
just close enuf me to feel a sort of radiant vibration that
has that ever enchanting call to come closer. Closer I go
and we grapple, not in the sense of wrestlers, but in the
feeling that each are desirious of seeing which can get the
closer. The larger has his head bowed just a little and the
smaller has hers upwerd. Without a word being spoken things
happen and suddenly a kindred glow radiates thru and thru and
after many seconds of almost breathless contact their contact
releases slightly and Daddly quietly whispersMamma Dear you
are the sweetest, most precious Darling in the world.Darling
these moments that I hold you so close and almost check your
breathing are the sweetest moments of my life,- I love them
more than you realize but not more than you love them I hope.
Wish you were present this very moment for I could well afford
to revive my sleepy self by giving you a dozen. I love you.
Lola, Dr. The babies and Tubbie are fine and when
I see Dr. put his arms around Lola and kiss her I get so darn
lonesome for My mamma that I scarcely know how to contain
myself. To love is wonderful and especially to love someone so
devotedly as I do. Did you say how longI should have to continue to be away from My Mamma? Hope not very long.
Today is very cool in fact the winter clothes
feel good. Quite cloudy with the sun peeping thru occasionally
Not a day to blister but one to remind you that this is only
the beginning of what is to follow. I hope we can be going
south long before it expresses itself in that snowey blanket.

DR. W. D. BROADHURST
Douglass Physician
THE IDAHO FIRST NATIONAL BUILDING
CALDWELL, IDAHO

Have a chance to sell the Caldwell home, but gosh Honey when I think of selling our very home I get cold feet. Needless to say if theyget enuf money which they haven't as yet, I presume they will get it. According to realestate men they have had many inquiries regarding the stock ranch, but as yet no one has come along with enuf money to give a good subsantial payment. Should much rather sell the stockranch than the home place. I'll ask My Mamma before I sell our home, and whatever she says we will do, cause I love her very much and respect your judgment.

Never found a bit of lipstick on the whole trip home other than a Lieutenant in the Waves and of course since she was an officer she sort of held herself a little highhat. Friendly but she ate her own lipstick,- I guess that is where it goes when it disappears without the aid of other lips. Not bad to eat when I am getting itt at home but this boarding house stuff I sort of resent it very much. Better send me a nice big red juicy one for my lunch. Please Honey.

Hope to go to the stockranch Tuesday and shall talk to bernard about riding for cattle or what he thinks will be the best time. I hope we can ride this month for it usually gets cold and stormy in October. Besides if the grazing dept. will give me an extended range lease I am going to sell them all.Shall keep you posted as to my intentions.

Have had many inquiries regarding my going elk hunting, but since I know not when we round the cattle up, I can give nothing definite to anyone. I may not even go for if we are away this winter then the meat would be of no value other than the good I derive from the trip.I love to go even tho I should have to give the meat away.

Reintstated the insurance on the car today so if it is wrecked now our liability so for as public liability will be taken care of. I think the policy holds clauses regarding property damage as well.

Am so sleep that I must go lie down for a few moments and all the time I'll be thinking of the Dearest Little Mommie in the world. Honey do write often for I get so lonesome for you that I hardly know what to do. Must go so with all my love and more I am your lonesome,sleepy

Daddy Husband.

Gladys to Willis, September 8th. Another torn up letter from the heat vent:

Postmark: Truckee, CA 9/10/46
Sunday
Darling:
It was sweet of you to write me the nice long letter from Winn. Thanks.

I am lonely without you – to hear from you so soon is a pleasure – I worried much as I knew your cold was not too good. I also … bus riding.

I stayed in bed Friday & Sat as my cold has sprouted into quite an affair. Jess was up today & took me for a brief ride. He surely was surprised to see me & told me … happy too I could remain longer. If … dear … to let me stay. I do feel piggy like about the car, but am glad I can come home when & as quickly as I get things straight here. May have to make one trip to Sacramento. I'm sorry your visit was so short & not too pleasant. I'd hoped you would have a really lovely time (Darn me) uh? Next time be better.

Gwynn goes to the Dr. Thursday. She isn't doing right. I'm afraid she is going to have a miscarriage. … Pat has two new infections & has hourly shots of penicillin. Some hospital we have here. Every one sick but … looks …

Do hope you will try not to worry too much or to be too lonely. Once I get this all done here I won't have

to come back. Wow, it's been a most
trying time.

Just got lunch … Gwyns in bed so
may … & I close … joint from Luke …
for slept every …

It's been warmer darling, really
hot to …

Honey dear, I'll write more
tomorrow, my head … so from sinus …
scarcely …

I miss you,
Your loving Mommie

The next letter is from W.D. to Gladys, September 9th.
She and Alvin have now been gone for 5 weeks:

Postmark dated: Sept, 9, 1946 - 5:00
PM - Boise, Idaho
Addressed to: Gladys Broadhurst, Box
625, c/o Big Chief Camp, Truckee, CA

Hotel Owyhee
C. F. MANN, MANAGER
Boise, Idaho

4 P.M.

Darling:

So happy to hear your sweet voice
& to know the cold was better instead
of worse. Didn't want you to catch my
cold but just one of those things.

Darling under separate cover I am
mailing you a little token of love
& hope you enjoy them. Personally I
like spicy color & trust you do.

Am also sending Gwen & Tony a
little pillow. Had thot of a couple

of initialed towels, but try to buy such a thing in Boise. Ow!

I love you & hope that full recovery in every way will come soon for I so want to see My Darling well & happy. Naturally when you are well & happy I am the same for what effects you likewise effects me - believe it or not. This is perfectly natural for two peas in a pod can not grow & thrive if one is disturbed. I love you.

Sorry you are having trouble with the car. However, things happen to them even in spite of careful handling. Anyway it is insured against property damage & public liability, so I feel much safer & more at ease.

Have been all afternoon with the grazing board trying to get them to grant me a holding field on Juniper Mt. That is a place to hold cattle while rounding up. They have finally granted same after months of wrangling. Thanks to them as this privilege materially helps the stock ranch.

Gosh I would give a million to hold you in my arms & tell you I love you, but just to talk to you helps me to bare that lonesomeness until you return.

Shall learn from Bernard about the best time to gather the cattle & advise you of same.

If possible am going to try to get the fall barley planted by Friday nite & be home for that call.

Must drop Tony & Gwen a note & mail your package & then head homeward.

I love you & adore you & miss you
ever & ever more.
Your lonesome Daddy.
All my love
Darling

W.D. to Gladys, September 15th:

Mailed via: Air Mail
Mailed to: Gladys Broadhurst
c/o Big Chief Camp
Box 625
Truckee, CA

Postmark:Caldwell, ID - Sep 16, 1946

Letterhead:Dr. W. D. BROADHURST
Drugless Physician
THE IDAHO FIRST NATIONAL BUILDING
CALDWELL, IDAHO

Sunday P.M.
My Most Darling Mommie:
    It was a perfect day other than
having a little rain & quite cool.
Dr., Lola, the kids, Tubbie & I drove
to Idaho City, Lowman & to Garden
Valley & then home. Honestly Honey the
Mts. & scenery were the most beautiful
ever. Now had my Honey been along my
happiness would have been sealed with
a seal that is the finest ever. I love
you adore you & miss you more than
ever. Darling I know how you love the
things I love & then when I have to try
to enjoy them without you, life just
doesn't seem right. You & you alone
answer the complement that has been
starving since I kissed the three of

you goodbye in Burley. Naturally we had drifted apart in person, but the moment I kissed those sweet lips in the Senator Hotel, my love a thousand strong flashed into full blossom.

Of course I fully understand, the trying moments you have gone thru & every moment of that time you have had the spirit of your most ardent lover & husband as fully & complete as I know how to give. I have tried never to fail you, in giving you the best I have, in spirit, soul, love, car, money & time. If I have failed in my shortcomings it has been only because I have not understood & not because I wanted to mar one moment of our past, present, or future happiness. Darling, I trust you see the same as I in this lite.

Naturally, loving you as I do, I so envy every moment of lost time. I fully realize that it was best for you to settle your problems in your field of knowledge. But regardless of time, I can only hope that from it all comes a bigger & better understanding & a confidence that has no parallel. Surely, I have been very much troubled, lonesome & almost lost, but not for a split second have I ever doubted that all will be O.K. when you have settled your present difficulties. I love you.

Am meeting with Mr. Sloan from Ontario tomorrow a.m. & he is bringing a prospective buyer for the stockranch. Was offered $48,000 for the home place today, but said little as I feel that neither you or I want to sell our beautiful home. From it all I get a lot of joy & know you will once you get well & feel its beauty. Shall we sell it or keep it for our nest egg? I'd naturally say keep it so we will always have a beautiful home. When we dispose of this where could we go to find anything that has any more value to us? Don't sell it Daddy? O.K.

Red is having a sale next Friday & have thot much about selling most of the furniture stored there. We do not need it here & as for the stockranch it has plenty for sale.

Will now know definitely until sometime this week when we will ride Juniper, but I am hoping soon as I want those cattle gathered so I can dispose of them.

George Vogt sold his ranch today for $25,000, the first place north of our home. I think it also included the 15 acres of Bonner's just north of him. However, the 40 acres sold for $25,000. Not bad.

Supper time so must eat a bite & always rember that you have a very lonesome Daddy with arms wide open for his Darling Wiffie just as soon as she feels that she can get away. I love you Darling. Dr.

Willis to Gladys, September 19th. Unknown to him, Gladys and Alvin were married two days ago:

Mailed via: Regular Mail
Mailed to: Gladys Broadhurst
Big Chief Camp

Box 625
Truckee, CA

Postmark:Caldwell, ID - Sep 20, 1946
Letterhead:Dr. W. D. BROADHURST
Drugless Physician
THE IDAHO FIRST NATIONAL BUILDING
CALDWELL, IDAHO

Sept. 19 - 46

My Darling:
 Received letter & card & thanks
a million for just a note from you
always give me a lot of joy. Send them
often. Naturally I should much prefer
to have you in person, but since that
doesn't seem possible for the moment,
then your sweet messages must suffice.
 Drove Mr. & Mrs. Housen from Parma
into the stockranch today. Drove to
Cliffs & then back & all over the ranch
in Jordan. Am asking $60,000 for the
ranch minus the cattle. May have to
take less, but I am going to sell it.
 Bulldozer is cleaning the creek so
that is going to be quite an expense.
This, however, will all be added to
the price.
 Plenty of chances to sell the
cattle, but am hoping that I can get
them all gathered before I have to
sell them. They are surely beautiful.
Wish you could see them. Better if
you felt well enuf to do some riding
with me & really get the feel of the
wide open spaces. Someday I hope.
 Had quite a heavy frost late
nite, but does not seemed to have hurt

the flowers to badly. They are really beautiful.

So you had snow & how in the world could you keep from freezing to death, without your Daddy? I'll bed you have moved to the house or something. Well I wish you were here so I could keep you nice & warm: Someday, soon, I hope.

Going into the stockranch early tomorrow a.m. & then back to Red's to help him with his sale. However, Grace is supposed to take her little lot & move just as soon as the sale is over. Feel sorry for her but she is too weakminded to warrant wedded bliss.

Realld do not know how much of that furniture to sell for if we sell the Jordan Valley ranch we do not need any of it. So guess it all goes.

Bernard & Fay told me about the strange man being in the house the night I left. They came close to getting up & chasing him in the car but they knew he would hide & get away. I just smiled & said nothing as they do not know I came to see you. Fay told me she had rec'd a card from you & was very happy with same. Thanks for thinking of her.

Lola told me today that she had written you & surely wanted to feel that this was your home & that she loved you very much. She also stated that just as soon as we wanted our home that they would gladly move. Such a kind heart.

Now Mamma Dear, I love you so much,
& honestly Honey, I often feel that I
can not live another day without you
but guess I'll have to grow stronger
& keep on hoping that soon we can
laugh & love together, I do love you.
To be hearing soon & often Your
lonesome Daddy,
Dr. Broady

W.D. to Gladys, September 20th. Gladys and Alvin have been gone for 2 days under 7 weeks, and they actually arrive in Ontario the night before W.D. mails this letter.

DR. W. D. BROADHURST
Drugless Physician
THE IDAHO FIRST NATIONAL BUILDING
CALDWELL, IDAHO

Saturday 20, 1946.

Dearest Honey:

Went into the sale early yesterday am and
after I arrived found that Red had changed the date of
sale till next Tuesday. However, I gathered the things I
felt I wanted to keep other than the dishes and then came
back to the valley for I had promised a prospective rentor
that I would be over to see him. Called and he had a much
better setup than I had anticipated. He has around $18,000
worth of fine equiptment and his crops are beautiful.He
is desirious of renting and I think he would be fine but
again one never knows anything about anybody until they
have lived and learned. I have that well of every rentor
that ever farmed the place only to find that after they
get on there then they do as they please and anything I
say means just so much hotair. However, if he will farm
for me as he is farming for the other fellow then I see no
reason why things would not be fine. I hope.
From all I know now Red, Bernard and I will
ride the range starting next week after the sale which is
Tuesday. Red and Bernard have a fairly good knowledge of
that country and one has to have or else he can easily get
lost. That could happen to me as but never having been that
way I little fear such a thing for I well know that going
down I'll come out somewhere.
I had so hoped that I could have had a real
vacation or at least enuf time to have gone hunting, but
now with several prospective buyers for the stockranch and
cattle and the riding, I doubt if I'll get to go. Dr. is
going with George Vogt and the party stands ready to take
me if only I could make arrangements which look out at this
writing. If I give this trip up it will be the first season
in 15 years and that is something. It is something that I
love and always seems to so helpful to me in every way.
May get to go later but then the weather si much colder
and a lot more hardships.
Katherine had cramps yesterday and Rudy in-
timated that he should be glad to have me come over and
look her over, but I kept mum for I certainly do not feel
that they are deserving of of my help since they have been
so cheap in everyway. Hope she is better which I feel sure
she will be.
So happy to learn that you were thinking about
coming home as your Daddy has been so lonesome and really
unhappy for his Mamma. Gosh Darling it seems as long as the
20 years that have passed from our parting in Burley. Altho
it has been not quite 2 months it seems years. Naturally
if I didn't love you so much, I could have borne your

DR. W. D. BROADHURST
Drugless Physician
THE IDAHO FIRST NATIONAL BUILDING
CALDWELL, IDAHO

being away with much more dignity, but when I love I love
with a sincerity that is difficult to describe. I know
how I feel but having experienced the feelings once be-
for in my life, I'll survive it all and altho battered
and worn from the experience I may emerge a stronger and
better man. Needless to say it isn't one that I should
care to experience often in my life, but since it had to
be I'll pass it and hoard it among my souveniors. Darling
you mean so much to me and I love you the mosta of anything in the world.
        I sometimes feel that possibly I bore you to
tears with my constant barrage of I love you and you are
the dearest thing in the world, but if such a thing should
ever happen, never be afraid to shout enuf and your Daddy
will try to refrain in words even tho he may still whisper
to you in the silence. Again that old open book just dying
for expression and always wanting M² Mamma to know that
there is no one in the whole wide world that means a
a thing me other than as friends. I love you Darling.
ENUF of this bunk and frogive me Darling for I write just
just as I feel even tho I can not express it is person.
        I am still hoping and looking forward to that
real honeymoon with the finest little lady in the the wide
open spaces and shall never be content to anything this
side of that for certainly we have never had a chance to
even know the most infinitesmal part of the store of real
life that wwaits us both if only this opportunity ever
expresses itself. You may feel different about it all but
until I know I still assume that this is correct.
        Am meeting some fellows from Ontario at eleven
so guess I better quit chattering and go my way and hoping
that I'll see you soon I am

                        Your loving Daddy,
                        Dr. Broady.

Alvin to Gene Ralphs, Sept. 24th. This is the only letter
we have that was written by Alvin.

Sept 24, 1946
Caldwell, Ida

Dear Red and Elsie,

Well I haven't got much to do so
I will write you a line. Gladys and I
got home all in one piece, we never
had any trouble of any kind so I guess
we were quite fortunate.

Have you got you a job yet, I am
not working at the present. I had a
chance to take another chauffeur job,
for 12 dollars a day and board. I
was supposed to drive a big gambler
around, he is from Las Vegas, Nevada.
I told him to go to hell. I had all
the chauffeur job I wanted. Oh, you
can see a lot of country while you are
driving (he said), I told him I didn't
care if I never saw any country, I
just didn't want the damned job. I
thought he was going to hang one on to
me, but he didn't. Swell I got home 2
days to late to ride roundup for Doc,
he hired another guy. I picked up a
job for $1.00 an hour that I think I
will start on tomorrow. I may go back
and cut Christmas trees for Tony and
Gwyn after while. And again I may go
to Green River Utah and go to work for
my uncle he is State supervisor and
road engineer or something like that

he wrote and said that I could get on if I would come down.

We stopped and saw your aunt & uncle Frank, in Winnemucca they are all well. Frank got his 20 year pin from the railroad. He wasn't working the day we stopped there. It was his birthday so he had a birthday surprise, we had a late breakfast with him.

Your aunt said that she hoped he didn't have to work that night she wanted to take him to a show. We left about 3 oclock so I don't no if she got to take him or not. I wish that you could see Gladys now you wouldn't know her, she is dieing by inches, she is thin and pale and looks as if she had lost 15 or 20 pounds since she has been home. She is living with a man she don't love and can't get her …
(Remainder of letter not found)

APPENDIX 2 – DOCUMENTS OF INTEREST

Below is one of the most puzzling items found in the poinsettia box. It is a copy of a Brand Registration Certificate for Mrs. Gladys Broadhurst dated March 29, 1946. This was almost two months prior to there even <u>being</u> a Mrs. Gladys Broadhurst. Note also that this certificate was mailed from the Bureau of Brands to the Caldwell address three months before Gladys arrived there for the first time.

Did Gladys register this brand in her name even before she married the doctor? How could she have done that and have it mailed to the Caldwell ranch without anyone else knowing about it? Is it possible that W.D. had already decided to marry Gladys in March and registered a brand in her name as a gift or surprise for her? Maybe this would be his wedding gift to her. I have found no mention of the brand in any of the correspondence or documents found so far.

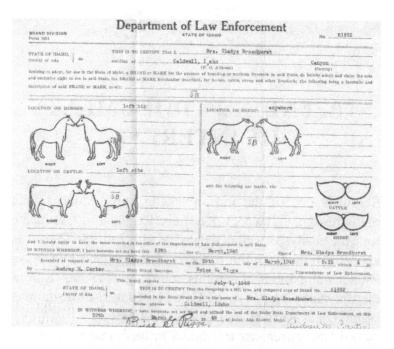

Below is the text of the will of Gladys' aunt Mary Ralphs Johnson. It is believed that Gladys fabricated this will. However, one curious aspect of this will is that Gladys inherits $350,000 provided she is married to Leslie Merle Lincoln. It also states the major part of her estate on Oahu go to Gladys and Leslie. It says nothing about three million dollars.

Perhaps this made-up will was for Leslie's benefit and she created another one for W.D.'s benefit. Or maybe she just started with this will and every time she told the story it was changed to fit her circumstances, growing larger each time she talked about it.

```
COPY

Wahiawa Heights
T.H.
November 26, 1944
```

I, Mary Johnson, being of sound
mind & my own free agent, do hereby
bequeath one year after my death to
Gladys E. Lincoln & Leslie Merle
Lincoln the major part of my estate
now on the island of Oahu T. H.
- providing Gladys E. Lincoln &
Leslie Merle Lincoln are man & wife
at the time of bequeath. $350,000
is in trust fund to be given only
to Gladys Lincoln & Leslie Merle
Lincoln. $5,000 goes to each of
her brothers - Jesse W. Ralphs,
Sterling Ralphs, Eugene B. Ralphs, &
Clifford Ralphs, - Mr. Charles Munson
is appointed Administrator, legal
resident of Oahu. E. T. Carter is
Representative at San Francisco.
To all others having claim on me I
leave the sum of One dollar $1.00.
This is my tru and last testament.

Mary Ralphs Johnson

Witness Charles A. Munson
Witness Ester Coulter.

Telegram from WD to Gladys 08-25-1945 – State's
Exhibit 64:

S51 10= =CALDWELL IDA AUG 25 1945 201P

GLADYS RALPHS =LINCOLN=   1945 AUG 25 PM 1 30
    411 SOUTH 7 ST TAFT CALIF=

=SAME ADDRESS DR W D BROADHURST CALDWELL IDAHO= BEST WISHES=
    DR W D =BROADHURST=

State v Broadhurst
State's Exhibit 64
Iden
admitted

Marriage Certificate, W.D. Broadhurst and Gladys
Lincoln – State's exhibit 31:

Marriage Certificate

State of Nevada } ss.
County of Washoe

212894

This is to Certify that the undersigned __Wm McKnight District Judge__

__Washoe County Nevada__ _did, on the_

__20th__ _day of_ __May__ _A. D. 19_ __46__ _join in lawful Wedlock_

__W.D. BROADHURST__ _of_ __Caldwell__

State of __Idaho__ _and_ __GLADYS LINCOLN__

of __Sacramento__ State of __California__ _with their_

mutual consent in the presence of __Bessie Ellsworth__ _and_

__Fred Lutgens__ _who were witnesses._

__Wm. McKnight__

__District Judge__

Recorded at the request of __Judge Wm. McKnight__ _Filed_ __MAY 22__, 19 __46__

__Delle B. Boyd__
County Recorder

State of Nevada } ss.
County of Washoe

I, __Delle B. Boyd__ _County Recorder in and for Washoe County, do_

hereby certify that I have compared the foregoing with the original record thereof as the same appears in my

office, in vol. __"114"__ _of Marriages, page_ __136__ _and that the foregoing document is a full,_

true and correct transcript therefrom, and of the whole of such original record.

WITNESS my hand and official seal hereunto set this __21st__ _day of_ __JAN__ _A. D. 19_ __47__

Delle B. Boyd
County Recorder

_By_ _____
Deputy Recorder

State vs Broadhurst
State's Exhibit 31
Iden.

ACSO OF NEV.

Check given by Willis to his new bride on their wedding day:

After Gladys has been gone to California for 4 weeks, W.D. is searching for answers on how to deal with her drug addiction. He solicits advice from a doctor in New York:

EDWARD SPENCER COWLES, M. D.
591 PARK AVENUE
BET. 63RD & 64TH STREETS
NEW YORK 21, N. Y.
RHINELANDER 4-7070

September 6, 1946

Dr. W. D. Broadhurst
Caldwell
Idaho

My dear Dr. Broadhurst:

The medication that we use in the treatment of functional disorders is phenobarbital, ½ grain, in the morning, at dinner time, and on going to bed; and eight teaspoonsful of Atop, once a day, in water. You may obtain the Atop through the Lustol Company, 675 Madison Avenue, New York City.

The medication is intended to put the nerve cells in splints. It is not in sufficient quantity to swamp the nerve cell but just enough to remove the irritability and to allow the nerve cell to take up its nourishment. It also stabilizes the emotions while the patient learns more about his feelings, not to push them down, but to make them come up. You must see the patient every day and give him the Atop yourself, while by re-education and suggestion you explain to him about the sensations in his body that he is misinterpreting.

Very truly yours,

Edward Spencer Cowles

Edward Spencer Cowles, M.D.

ESC:CM

Marriage certificate, Alvin & Gladys (Note that she made sure it was a different judge than the one who performed the wedding for her and W.D.) – State's exhibit 33:

Marriage Certificate

State of Nevada } ss.
County of Washoe

223697

This is to Certify that the undersigned **district judge** _____ did, on the

17th day of **September** A. D. 19 **46** join in lawful Wedlock

ALVIN L WILLIAMS of **Elko**

State of **Nevada** and **ELAINE HAMILTON**

of **Elko** State of **Nevada** with their

mutual consent in the presence of **V. Whitehead** and

Wm A Kelly who were witnesses.

A J Maestretti

District Judge

Recorded at the request of **Judge A. J. Maestretti** Filed **SEP 24** 19 **46**

Delle B. Boyd
County Recorder

State of Nevada } ss.
County of Washoe

I, **Delle B. Boyd** _____, County Recorder in and for Washoe County, do

hereby certify that I have compared the foregoing with the original record thereof as the same appears in my

office, in vol. **"121"** of Marriages, page **99** and that the foregoing document is a full,

true and correct transcript therefrom, and of the whole of such original record.

WITNESS my hand and official seal hereunto set this **21st** day of **JAN** A. D. 19 **47**.

Delle B. Boyd
County Recorder

By _____
Deputy Recorder

State n Broadhurst
State n Exhibit 33
John Adm

Warrant for the arrest of Gladys Broadhurst:

No. 140. WARRANT FOR ARREST—FELONY   Printed and for Sale by West Coast Ptg. & Bdg. Co., Portland, Or.

In Justice Court for ONTARIO District

STATE OF OREGON,   Malheur County, State of Oregon.
County of MALHEUR   } *ss.*

In the Name of the State of Oregon:

To THE SHERIFF OR ANY CONSTABLE OF THE COUNTY OF MALHEUR GREETING:

Information upon oath having been this day laid before me that the crime of Murder in the first degree

has been committed, and accusing Gladys Broadhurst *thereof.*

You are therefore hereby commanded to arrest the above named Gladys Broadhurst

and bring her *before me at* Ontario,

in said County, or in case of my absence or inability to act, before the nearest or most accessible

magistrate in this County.

Dated at Ontario, Oregon, *this* 19th *day of* October, *A. D. 19*46.

                 Justice of the Peace.
Ontario District, Malheur County, Oregon.

Will of Willis D. Broadhurst:

Probate Court, Canyon County,
Idaho
FILED OCT 25 1946
B R Riordan   Clerk

LAST WILL AND TESTAMENT

OF

WILLIS D. BROADHURST

＊ ＊ ＊ ＊

KNOW ALL MEN BY THESE PRESENTS: That I, WILLIS D.
BROADHURST, of Caldwell, Canyon County, Idaho, of the age of
fifty-one (51) years, or thereabouts, being of sound and disposing mind and memory and not acting under duress, menace,
fraud, or undue influence of any person or persons, whatso-
ever, do make, publish and declare this My Last Will and Testament, in the manner and form as follows, to-wit:

FIRST: I direct that my Executrix hereinafter named,
as soon as she shall have sufficient funds in her possession,
shall pay the expenses of my last sickness and death and all
of my just debts, and that as a part of the expense of my
last sickness and death she shall place a marker at the head
of my final resting place.

SECOND: I give, devise and bequeath all the rest,
residue and remainder of my estate, whether real estate or
personal property, and wheresoever situated, to my beloved
wife, GLADYS ELAINE BROADHURST.

THIRD: I do not intend to give anything from my said
estate to any of my brothers or sisters, or to any of my
other relatives. It is my desire that they shall receive

Willis D. Broadhurst

RECORDED IN Will BOOK
3 AT PAGE 309   -1-
B R Riordan
PROBATE JUDGE

nothing from my estate.

FOURTH: I hereby make, constitute and appoint my wife, GLADYS ELAINE BROADHURST, the Executrix of this My Last Will and Testament and direct that no bond shall be required of her for the faithful performance of any of her duties as Executrix of this My Last Will and Testament.

FIFTH: I direct that my said Executrix shall have authority with or without the interference of a court of competent jurisdiction to sell, mortgage, hypothecate, or encumber any of my estate whenever it shall be necessary to do so, and that she shall have authority to make, execute, acknowledge and deliver any mortgages, deeds, indentures, notes, checks and any and all other instruments that may be necessary or proper to carry out this clause of my said Will.

SIXTH: I hereby revoke all former Wills by me made.

IN WITNESS WHEREOF, I have hereunto set my hand and seal this 25 day of September, A. D., 1946.

Willis D. Broadhurst (SEAL)

* * * * *

The foregoing instrument, consisting of three (3) pages, including the page upon which the attestation clause is concluded, was, at the time and date thereof, by WILLIS D.

-2-

BROADHURST, the maker thereof, signed in our presence and in the presence of each of us, and at the time of his subscribing said instrument he declared that it was his LAST WILL AND TESTA-MENT, and at his request and in his presence, and in the presence of each of us, and in the presence of each other, we have sub-scribed our names as witnesses thereto on the day and date specified in the said Will as the date on which the same was made.

NAME	ADDRESS
Mildred Kinsey	Caldwell, Idaho
Cleve Groome	Caldwell Idaho

APPENDIX 3 – PHOTOS

Poinsettia Box

Willis D. Broadhurst – State's Exhibit 2

Gladys Broadhurst

The Oregonian:

AP Wirephoto:

Alvin Lee Williams
Newspaper unknown:

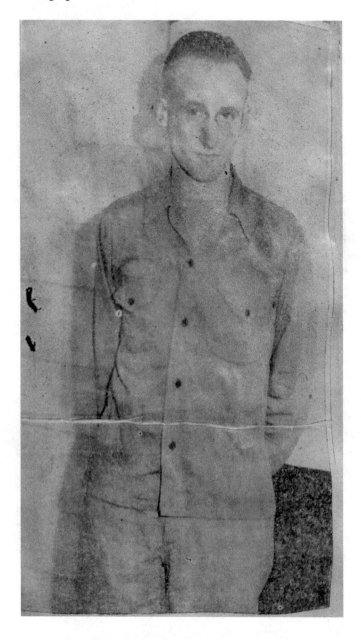

Leslie Lincoln - State's Exhibit 53:

Purported Photo of Lester Lincoln – State's Exhibit 6

Written on back: *1st Lt. Lester Melvin Lincoln*
Les' twin brother

Gladys' defense team. Left to Right are Cleve Groome, D. D. DeCoe, William Langroise and PJ Gallagher:

Dr. Floyd Adams, Lola Adams, Blaine Hallock & D.A. Charles Swan (left to right)

Broadhurst Trial Enters Seventh Day

Most of Second Week May Be Consumed By Prosecution

VALE, Ore. (special) — The trial of Gladys Broadhurst on first-degree murder charges, with the state asking the death penalty, goes into its seventh day here today.

The state so far has managed to complete introduction of evidence which shows a murder was committed—that Dr. W. D. Broadhurst, the defendant's husband, was slugged over the head and shot with a shotgun at a lonely spot on the ION highway 15 miles north of Jordan Valley.

Alvin Lee Williams, Mrs. Broadhurst's chauffeur and sometimes called by her 'My Man Friday,' is said to have signed a confession to the killing.

The state claims that Mrs. Broadhurst, who allegedly married Williams under an assumed name in Reno after she married Dr. Broadhurst, inspired Williams in the commission of the crime.

The state says it will prove:

1. Mrs. Broadhurst conceived a deliberate scheme to do away with Broadhurst so she would inherit his wealth.

2. She caused him to make his will, leaving his entire estate to her, little more than two weeks before he was slain.

Key witnesses in the case of the State of Oregon versus Gladys Broadhurst charged with complicity in first degree murder in the slaying of her husband, the late Dr. W. D. Broadhurst, are shown here with prosecuting attorneys. At left is Dr. F. L. Adams, Caldwell chiropractor and nephew of Dr. Broadhurst with whom the murdered man resided at the time of his death; Mrs. Adams, whose sensational testimony regarding the conduct of Mrs. Broadhurst and her alleged conspirator was given in court Wednesday; Blaine Hallock, Baker, Oregon attorney and special prosecutor, and Malheur County District Attorney Charles W. Swan. The picture was taken just after Mrs. Adams had left the stand Wednesday evening following an hour and a half of testimony.

(Unknown newspaper)

APPENDIX 4

MEN GLADYS RALPHS MARRIED

(Note: Gladys Ralphs was born 6/25/1906)

1. 5/19/1927 - William Bacel Hendricks
   a. Married in Minidoka, ID
   b. Gladys June Ralphs is 20 years old, a few weeks short of turning 21

2. 8/6/1928 - Albert Earnest Richardson, age 23
   a. Married in Logan, Cache County, UT
   b. Married by a judge at the courthouse, the same day the license was issued
   c. Miss Gladys Ralphs is 22

3. 1/30/1939 - Carroll M. Anderson, age 31
   a. Married in Reno
   b. Gladys Elaine Ralphs is 32, but she listed her age as 30

4. 6/9/1940 - Virgil D. Warner (perhaps Virgil T. Warner), age 28
   a. Married in Reno
   b. A large wedding with many guests, including Nevada Governor E.P Carville and his wife
   c. Miss Gladys Ralphs is 33, a few weeks shy of 34

5. 1/28/1942 – Leslie Merle Lincoln, age 24
   a. Married in Fort Ord, CA
   b. Married by an army chaplain with two witnesses
   c. Gladys Elaine Ralphs is 35, but she listed her age as 32

6. 5/19/1946 – Willis David Broadhurst - 51
   a. Married in Reno
   b. Gladys E. Lincoln is 39

7. 9/17/1946 - Alvin Lee Williams - 23
   a. Married in Reno
   b. Elaine Hamilton (Gladys) is 40
   c. She used the false name Elaine Hamilton

8. 5/2/1961 - Leo John O'Shea - 57
   a. Married in Marion County, OR
   b. Gladys is 54

ENDNOTE

With the goal of providing readers the exact text of the various letters and the trial transcript, please note that the errors in quoted texts were carried forward into this book, and thus are the errors of the original authors and not of the author of this book. A good example of this is in the letter from Willis dated 9/15/1946 where he calls her his "Wiffie." In other letters he spells it "Wifie."

ACKNOWLEDGEMENTS

I would like to give my heartfelt thanks to the following who aided greatly in the creation of this book:

1. <u>Mary A. Jenkins</u>, Paroled Offender Information Request Specialist, Oregon Department of Corrections. She gave me some of the most helpful early information, including the "Sentence Data Record" from the Oregon State Penitentiary, which gave the ID numbers, dates of birth and dates of parole of both Gladys and Alvin. This is information I had been unable to find until then, and proved extremely helpful in the research process.

2. <u>Phillip Margolin</u>, NY Times best-selling author who graciously encouraged me and gave me suggestions on where to focus my research.

3. <u>Rebecca Scott</u>, Newsroom Assistant, Southern Oregon Media Group, who sent me a copy of the article dated 10/14/1949 in the *Medford Mail Tribune* about an attorney asking to be appointed Gladys' guardian.

4. <u>Stephanie Mendiola</u>, Malheur County Circuit Court, who searched their records thoroughly to find a copy of the trial transcript. When it turned out the transcript was not stored at Vale, she then referred me to the State Archives Division for further search.

5. <u>Dan Cummings</u>, Planning & Zoning Director, City of Ontario, who helped me with information about the family office building. He was very willing to help, has lived in Ontario for 40 years, and is interested in local history.

6.   Joanne Cunningham, the Curator of the Jordan Valley Museum, who very graciously searched for and found their scrapbook filled with newspaper articles about the murder and trial. She allowed me to photograph as many articles as I wished, which proved to be a treasure trove of information that was very helpful. Joanne was kind enough to come to the museum on a Sunday afternoon and open up to meet with Deb and me and allow us as much time as we needed to get our photos.

7.   Jill Miller, Ontario friend, who immediately suggested Borderline Personality Disorder when she heard the story I was about to write. This was a mental illness I had heard mentioned for years, but which I didn't really understand. The name, which clearly is a misnomer, suggests something minor. Once I researched it, BPD is definitely a severe mental illness and the actions of Gladys do indeed mirror the actions of people with this mental illness.

8.   The internet. There were three great sources of information in gathering the history of this crime: the trial transcripts, the newspaper articles from the Jordan Valley museum, and the internet. It is an amazing thing that today we can find a plethora of information on the internet about events that occurred 70 to 100 years ago. What a tool!

9.   Laura Stewart, a friend who read my first manuscript and was kind enough to provide several important suggestions.

10.   Richard D. Bank, Attorney, author and writing coach who was most encouraging and helpful at a critical time in the writing of this book. He is also a professor of publishing law and creative nonfiction at Rosemont College.

11.   My wife Deb, who encouraged me from the beginning and throughout the writing of this book, and very patiently put up with me focusing all my time and energy on writing the book. She also proofread the entire book and helped immensely. Thank you, Dear!

*To view the rest of the letters and more photos,
please visit: **wbp.bz/tildeathdousphotos***

*For More News About Patrick Gallagher,
Signup For Our Newsletter:*

http://wbp.bz/newsletter

*Word-of-mouth is critical to an author's long-term success. If you appreciated this book please
leave a review on the Amazon sales page:*

http://wbp.bz/tildeathdousa

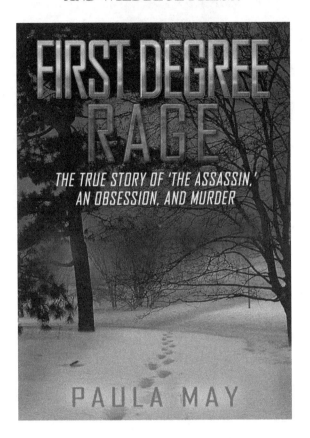

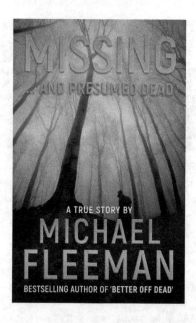

WILDBLUE
PRESS

See even more at:
http://wbp.bz/tc

More True Crime You'll Love From WildBlue Press

A MURDER IN MY HOMETOWN by Rebecca Morris

Nearly 50 years after the murder of seventeen year old Dick Kitchel, Rebecca Morris returned to her hometown to write about how the murder changed a town, a school, and the lives of his friends.

wbp.bz/hometowna

BETRAYAL IN BLUE by Burl Barer & Frank C. Girardot Jr.

Adapted from Ken Eurell's shocking personal memoir, plus hundreds of hours of exclusive interviews with the major players, including former international drug lord, Adam Diaz, and Dori Eurell, revealing the truth behind what you won't see in the hit documentary THE SEVEN FIVE.

wbp.bz/biba

SIDETRACKED by Richard Cahill

A murder investigation is complicated by the entrance of the Reverend Al Sharpton who insists that a racist killer is responsible. Amid a growing media circus, investigators must overcome the outside forces that repeatedly sidetrack their best efforts.

wbp.bz/sidetrackeda

BETTER OFF DEAD by Michael Fleeman

A frustrated, unhappy wife. Her much younger, attentive lover. A husband who degrades and ignores her. The stage is set for a love-triangle murder that shatters family illusions and lays bare a quiet family community's secret world of sex, sin and swinging.

wbp.bz/boda

CPSIA information can be obtained
at www.ICGtesting.com
Printed in the USA
BVHW041941151120
593384BV00017B/849

9 781952 225161